JUST OFF THE SWALE

First published by Meresborough Books, 1978

This updated edition published by Chaffcutter Books, 2004

ISBN 0 9532422-7-7

The Society for Spritsail Barge Research was established in 1963 by a band of enthusiasts concerned that the rapid decline and possible extinction of these splendid and historically significant craft would pass largely unrecorded. From the thousands of Thames sailing barges once plying the estuaries of the south-east and beyond, today just a handful survive in active commission, charter parties and business guests replacing the grain, cement and coal cargoes of yesteryear.

Now renamed The Society for Sailing Barge Research, reflecting a broadening interest in other allied types of craft, the Society organises walks, talks and exhibitions and publishes Topsail, a regular treasure chest of sailing barge history profusely illustrated with fascinating photographs of long lost craft and the ports they once served. Members also receive a twice yearly newsletter which highlights the fortunes of those barges which survive, as well as providing further snippits of our maritime heritage as ongoing research yields yet more of that trade, a way of life which from origins going back hundreds, even thousands of years, ceased in 1970 when the *Cambria* carried her last freight under sail alone.

Membership enquiries to Margaret Blackburn,
21 Newmarket Road, Stretham, Cambridgeshire CB6 3JZ

Published by
Chaffcutter Books, 39 Friars Road, Braughing, Ware, Hertfordshire SG11 2NN, England
in association with the Society for Sailing Barge Research

Printed and bound in Great Britain by
CPI Bath, Lower Bristol Road, Bath BA2 3BL, England

To Cecily

JUST OFF THE SWALE

Don Sattin

The story of the barge building village of Conyer

With illustrations by Jeremy Nesham

The Sidders Windmill on Conyer Bank.

CHAFFCUTTER

Acknowledgements

In preparing this book a lot of people have given me a great deal of their time and help. Most of them were known to me, others complete strangers. All gave their help ungrudgingly. To me they are part of this book, with their eagerness to answer my questions, to search their houses for old photographs, and to give up many hours of their valuable time. They urged me on when I was ready to give it all up.

Many times this manuscript was put aside when sources of information dried up. If all the avenues of research had a successful ending this book would have been much larger, but over the period of seven years more paper found its way into the waste paper bin than in ten volumes of the present size.

My long suffering wife, bless her, bore the inconvenience of late meals, the noise of my typewriter, piles of books and papers all over the house, in complete silence. To her I am most grateful.

For the final resting places of the Conyer built sailing barges I have to thank that well known barge historian Tom Redshaw who saved me many hours of research by compiling a list for me. I am also most grateful to Richard-Hugh Perks for the many hours he spent making this book readable.

Others that have given me constructive help are Pat Sillcock, Tina and Melvin Sillcock, and Jeremy Nesham who did the lovely drawings.

My thanks also to the staffs of the County Archives, Maidstone, and the National Maritime Museum at Greenwich.

Many people loaned me photographs which I have credited to them, for which I am most grateful. The original source of some photographs remains obscure, but I owe a debt to the bygone photographers for their valuable record of days gone by.

D.L.S.

Note

The Kent County Council Archives Office is located in the Records Building at County Hall, Maidstone. For anyone intending to search the records it is best to first write to the County Archivist about your intended visit, who will help you the best he can. The building has five floors, and each floor has four rooms, seventeen of these rooms are fitted with shelves and racking, three miles of it, holding approximately twenty million documents. There are catalogues to help find documents; even looking through these catalogues takes time so one must not be disappointed with one's results gained in a day's search.

Anyone wanting to see the Documents mentioned in this book need only to call in and ask for reference numbers quoted under:

Tithe award of Teynham (1841): (U857 Q17)
Revised Tithe Award (1863): (G/N/NPa 4/27)
Title Deeds: Oziers Barn Field, and use of Wharf at Conyer Quay for
       Brickmaking (1866-1867) (U36 T1312)
Title Deeds: Windmill at Conyer Quay (1762-1829) (U47/22 T151)
Title Deeds: Windmill at Conyer Quay (1828-1839) (U229 T262A)

Contents

Note: During the period covered by this book a variety of spellings for certain place and subject names is evident. For example Frognal is spelt with two 'l's on some maps and documents and with one on others. In this publication for clarity just one spelling is used throughout.

Forward

From being the foreman shipwright at the Conyer barge building yard to becoming the agricultural engineer of a modern fruit farm Donald Sattin's life has been concentrated around the rich farm lands and the tidal waterways which lie off the Kentish Swale. In that time he came to know the men, and women, who worked in the barge yard, the brickfields and on the land, the skippers and their mates who brought their barges up into the creek to load bricks for London, the farmers, the villagers, the yachtsmen and the visitors. From Martha Head, who sailed as mate aboard her husband's Thames barge, to 'Lord Haw-Haw', who was better known for other things, Donald has set down the stories of his villagers.

Conyer is an appealing waterside community. Its creekway provides moorings for yachts and small cruisers, its Street is flanked by terraces of new, white weatherboarded cottages which overlook the creek, and in the Dock, where barges once used to load cement, houseboats and housebarges lie alongside landscaped gardens. In the brickfields Conyer bricks are now again made by hand, and on the surrounds of the village are grasslands reclaimed from former marsh. In May time, over towards Teynham Street, the landscape is a sea of cherry blossom.

The world which Donald recalls from his boyhood days is very different from the way of life that might have been experienced in other places. Here people's lives were ruled by nature and by the tides - primitive lives. Work started before the sun came up and continued into the evening, with men tramping perhaps 4 miles to their places of work. And that work was hard. Imagine lying in freezing mud, under the bottom of a barge, driving home new spikes into the bottom timbers, with so little working space that there was hardly movement for the maul; or working for hours on end in the bottom of a saw-pit, guiding the saw, with the dust raining down into your eyes and hair.

It was a way of life in which women often worked in the brickfields, or sailed as mates to their husbands, and still found time to bring up strong families. It was a world, too, where punctuality was important. Donald prides himself that only twice in his life has he been late for work...and then only by one or two minutes.

But if the work was hard then so was the play. If bar counters could talk I warrant that the Barge Bar of the Ship Inn would have some merry tales to tell.

Half a century ago village life was much freer than it is today, so I am informed. Children swam in the stream or the creek, caught flat fish in their bare hands, and had the freedom to move around, without our present day restrictions and physical enclosures. They knew about wild life, flora and fauna, knew how to handle a boat, and grew up with a sense of pride. Pride was important in a village like Conyer, it was being proud of one's skills and craftsmanship, and being proud of the locally built sailing barges from Alfred Marconi White's yard. It was for these barges that Conyer will always have a special place in history - *Satanita*, *Westmoreland* and the famous racer *Sara*.

Village histories are not just part and parcel of the growing awareness people have for local communities, they also perform an essential function. Compositions of villages have changed since the Great War. There is no longer continuity among families and so stories of the past are no longer handed down from generation to generation as they used to be. Education in villages like Conyer used to be elementary to a degree not even envisaged by the authors of the education acts. History was not written, it was passed on by word of mouth, in the same way that knowledge and skills were handed down by the elders to the youngsters.

In 'Just Off The Swale' Donald Sattin records the memories of the people who can recall what life used to be like in a small waterfront community in the days of the horse and cart and the sailing barge.

Richard-Hugh Perks

Forward to this new edition

Researching local history is not a finite process; there is no great denouement for, like the iceberg, a significant proportion remains under the surface. The very printing of this book some quarter of a century past stirred the memories of a wider audience, and as a result many more photographs have come to light and a few more details of Conyer's past have emerged. Much of this material is included in the pages which follow.

What is also evident is the constant evolution of the lifestyle of the district, to the point where the first edition has in itself become a time warp, a snap-shot of an instant and a viewpoint of what had gone before. Now many of those people and enterprises that were changing the face of Conyer in the 1970s have gone. Passed away are those whose reminiscences formed the basis of much of the original text; with one exception that is, for the author still lives a stone's throw from where it all was, and takes an ongoing active interest in the history of the locality into his eighties.

Richard Walsh

Looking east towards the village of Conyer in 1968. The course of the old creek crosses the photograph about two-thirds down, that part to the left forming the tidal dock built by the brick and cement makers Richardsons in the mid 19th. century, that to the right little more than a drying ditch. Beyond the houses with long front gardens, the white roadside building was once the village centre pub, the Brunswick Arms.

Chapter 1

Just Off The Swale

Ask an old timer how you get to Conyer and he may probably tell you: 'Round the Island. Four Fathom Channel, Ham Gat into the East Swale - fetch up past Faversham Creek's mouth and Harty Ferry to South Deep, and Conyer Creek is on the port hand, inside Fowley Island.'

Of course, another may tell you differently. That the best way to Conyer is: 'Up Queenborough, under the Kingsferry Bridge - at Milton Creek keep on going to Fowley Island...'

Either way, you will find your way up to the Quay when the tide starts flooding into the Creek. For Conyer lies on a small winding waterway which leads from the Kentish Swale into what were once the unembanked marshlands. Ahead lies the Island of Sheppey; behind is the old Roman road from Rochester to Canterbury. In between are the winding creekways which served the marsh farms and the orchard lands of the Garden of England. On their banks were boat-building yards, brickfields and cement works; little communities which serviced the land and the sea.

The village of Conyer and the area which surrounded it was a very different place a hundred years ago, when this was an industrial place, and much of the land between the Creek's mouth and the railway line was covered with brickfields and washbacks. Then two horse-drawn tramways and a railway connected the brickfields with the wharves at Conyer Creek, while today these lands are planted to apple and cherry orchards. But although you can still see some of the remaining features of this industry, the Conyer of a thousand or even 2,000 years ago is now quite unrecognisable as it was so geographically different.

When the Romans came and settled this coastline, Conyer was a narrow peninsula of high ground jutting out into the Swale and the land to both East and West lay under water. In 1953 when the flood waters broke through the sea walls it was possible to see the extent of the coastline as it was in Roman days. The sea covered the whole area from the west side of Conyer as far as the high grounds at Tonge and Murston. On the east side the water stretched from Conyer to the high ground at Luddenham and Uplees. In places the peninsula on which Teynham Street and Conyer came to be built was less than a few hundreds yards wide. In each of the two bays flanking Conyer the Romans established ports. The bays were wide, sheltered from the wind by the surrounding high ground close to the rich cornlands, and favourable places from which to conduct trade.

The Romans established a pottery in what I term 'Luddenham Bay', and some years ago I uncovered pottery and other artifacts here which were authenticated by the Maidstone Museum. In Conyer village itself there was a Roman settlement where again remains have been uncovered, and there was probably a third settlement to the west of the village.

'Luddenham Bay' formed the estuary of the now lost river Lyn, and the valley of the Lyn ran south-west to a point between the villages of Lynsted and Norton. On its west side there were vineyards on the bank where Teynham Church came to be built in Norman times. But on the site of St. Mary's Church was formerly a much older settlement, and you can still see the flat red Roman tiles built into the walls of the church. In the churchyard, in front of the porch is a stone structure, like a high tomb, said to have been the original alter before the present Norman church was built.

Further to the west is Tonge where it is claimed the Hengist and Horsa begged from King Vortigern as much land as could be encompassed by the hide of a bull cut into thongs. There Tonge Castle was built and fortified.

In the first thousand years the geography of this region changed little. Then in Norman times a palace for the Archbishops of Canterbury was built between Teynham Church and Conyer village, and parts of the stone foundations can be remembered by the older folk in the village. Lanfranc and Stephen Langton were two of the Archbishops who inhabited the Palace. Hubert died here in 1205 and at the news of his death King John rejoiced saying he was 'never king (indeede) before this houre'. Of one Archbishop it was related that the household he kept was second only to that of the king.

Until early Norman times, the River Lyn was probably navigable as far as Lynsted. The estuary was a commonly used refuge, where ships came to shelter in bad weather anchoring off Teynham Street.

The port of Teynham was located just to the north-east of the church, by the village which is now known as Teynham Street. Just outside the Street, on the road to Deerton Street, the land follows the Causeway which bridges what once used to be the valley of the Lyn. This Causeway, nearly 200 yards long (and that will give you an idea of the width of the Lyn) was constructed for the Archbishops' Palace, to create a fresh water lake which was stocked with fish. Thus navigation was impaired above Teynham to Osiers Farm, where the River Lyn had narrowed.

It is said that the Causeway was constructed in the 11th. century, and at that time sea-walls were built along the edge of the shores to both bays. The natural flow of water was impeded and the problems which

Teynham was to suffer stemmed from this action. By the 14th. century the ague had come to Teynham. The village was abandoned, the port deserted and the whole physical geography of the region was altered.

What happened was that as the sea-walls encroached on the estuaries mud marshes formed, and to the seaward sides of them still more walls were built. But unlike the embankers of the 17th. and 18th. centuries the mediaeval wall builders had little knowledge of drainage. So when the mud, which had formed when the sea retreated, began to dry out fauna formed, and mosquitoes began to breed on the new marshes.

The result was mosquito infested lands from which came forth marsh gas and vapours. A heavy mist hung over the coastline and it became an unhealthy place in which to live.

The ague had come to North Kent, and on the shore lines of the Thames, Medway and Swale none but the marsh born could survive. In 1576 William Lambarde in his 'Perambulations of Kent' quotes the ditty:

'He that will not live long,
Let him dwell at Murston, Tenham or Tong.'

The villagers all but deserted Teynham and moved south to the line of the old Roman Road which came to be known as Greenstreet. The old side of Teynham gradually came to be re-occupied once the ague had been contained, and the village became known by its present name of Teynham Street, while today Greenstreet is erroneously called Teynham.

In 1533 one Richard Harris, who was fruiterer to Henry VIII purchased 105 acres of ground at Teynham, and planted apple trees and the sweet cherry which was imported from overseas. From this stemmed the Garden of England, a great plantation of fruit on the rich, brick earth lands.

Even before this time there was a demand for locally grown produce, vegetables, corn, barley and other cereals, which soon would no longer be produced in London in quantities sufficient to feed the population.

There was a need for a new port to serve Teynham and the surrounding district, to transport goods and passengers. It must be remembered that there were few roads then and travel overland was risky. Robbers and cut-throats often roamed around the countryside in bands, pillaging carts; so water travel was essential for safety's sake. The route to London lay via the Swale (inside the Isle of Sheppey) through the Medway, Yantlet Creek and Sea Reach, but there was now no suitable port at Teynham.

The River Lyn had dried into a narrow creekway with marshes either side, entering the East Swale between the present site of Luddenham Gut and Conyer, and was then no longer suitable for navigation. Conyer, on the east bank of the bay which had stretched as far as Tonge was the only suitable location.

The enwalling of the marshes left only a narrow channel to the west of Conyer. From Tong it wound its way past Blacketts and Conyer village to the delta mouth where there were at least four channelways around Fowley Island into the Swale. Fowley Island itself is something of a mystery. Originally it stretched, in a narrow band from opposite high ground, but instead of being part of the

Map labels: THE EAS(T) SWALE · The Hundred of Tenham · Blacketts · Conyers Key · HUNDRED · Great Backs · Little Backs · TENHAM · Freynal(?) · Barrow Green · BUCKLAND · 13 M. · TENHAM

This old map, which was published around 1798 and is believed to be one of Hasted's, shows a very different course to the creek as it is today.

Conyer peninsula it was probably an island in its own right, sticking out of the bay in the same way as Blacketts, like the Islands of Elmley and Harty on the north side of the Swale. It was bisected by at least one creek. Now very little of it remains, much was eroded away, the rest was dug out by the 'muddies' and taken to Conyer by barge to be used for brick making.

The date when Teynham Street on the River Lyn ceased to be used as a port and Conyer Quay came into being is not known, but the two probably existed side by side from the 13th. century onwards. On Marsh Lane, below the Causeway, you can still see the remains of an old wharf, and in the dried up bed of the River Lyn you can see the flat ground in front of it, where the mud was kept carefully luted and this wharf might have remained in use until the 17th. century, but by then the Town Quay had moved to Conyer.

The new creek twisted and turned across the marshes. It was difficult to navigate, with narrow entrances and a winding course which restricted usage.

In the 14th. century Conyer Creek was used by local shipping. These craft were known as 'Crayers', vessels of about 60 tons. In that century Thomas Jerome who owned a Conyer farm also owned a crayer, the *Elizabeth*, together with a 'Lyhter boat'. It is possible that crayers were unable to reach the village's wharves and that goods had to off-loaded and lightered up?

In the will of Thomas Peers, dated 1509, he left 'Quenes Quay' (Queens) with 'Frognal Flat' to his wife, and one John Peers was to have 'Half the landage there...'

'Quenes' Quay may have been next to the Ship Inn where Bird and then White were to have their barge yards. His Majesty enjoyed a right of way to the waters edge here. Most inconvenient, as it ran right through the middle of the sheds!

'Frognal Flat' probably referred to the flat land where a tributary from Conyer Creek ran up to Frognal.

In the 16th. century Teynham was referred to as a 'Toun', and the Toun Quay was located at Conyer. Later this became known as Parish Wharf, and this was in front of the Ship Inn. Even in the late 18th. century it was unpleasant to live in and around Conyer. Ireland in his 'History of the County of Kent' wrote:

'The air of this place is very unhealthy, from being situated contiguous to the marshes, so that the inhabitants are constantly affected with the Ague, as well as intermittent fevers, and are in general very short lived...'

Notwithstanding Ireland, St. Mary's churchyard demonstrates a contrary view - one of longevity. George Honeyball, father of Frederick, the victualler and coal merchant and grandfather of Colonel James Frederick, was born in 1785. He lived to be 91, his son to be 83 and his grandson to be 74. But alas poor George's wife was comparatively short lived. She only just made 90! Nevertheless, it was not until around 1800 the marshes became a healthier place to live and people gradually returned to Teynham Street and began to inhabit Conyer.

But, certainly in Ireland's time, Conyer's Quay was sufficiently important to attract much local industry and ship trades. He describes Conyer:

'...on a small Creek, in the marshes, is Conyer's Key, much used for the shipping of corn and goods from this part of the country; near which there is an oil mill, formerly the property of one 'Best'.'

In addition, although Ireland does not tell us, there were cornmills, including Sidders mill above where the Dock is now and Hinkley's mill on Marsh Lane, by the side of the dry valley of the Lyn. He doesn't mention bricks either. Probably the Romans had brickfields here and bricks must have been manufactured throughout the middle ages.

The 19th. century saw the start of the industrial expansion at Conyer. It hinged naturally around the brickmaking industry. The original fields were to the south of the quay, between there and Greenstreet, and as each field was worked out so fresh fields to the back came to be worked.

The demand for bricks during the prosperous mid to late 19th. century was insatiable. Conyer's accessibility to London by sailing barge and the local availability of the raw materials for brick making ensured success.

By the 1860s maps show the principle fields all to be near the railway line, quite some distance from Conyer. And that will give you an idea of how much land had been worked prior to that date.

From West to East, the Mercer family owned the Frognal Works, over towards Tong and this was connected to the west corner of Conyer Creek by means of a horse drawn tramway. Next to this at Frognal, was Millichamp & Chambers Brickworks (later owned by

The embankment which carried the tramways from the Frognal Works brickfield to Mercer's Wharf, pictured in 1976.

the 'Co-operative') who had a tramway running parallel to Mercer's, culminating at their wharf which is now the site of Jarman's Boatyard. The Richardson family owned the Top Field which was connected to the Dock at Conyer by a railway line. On the course of the line, which later became a tramway, you can see the pump where Richardson's steam locomotive filled up with water. At Top Field, now an orchard, as with other fields in this part of Teynham, the wheelwrights shop still remains, but the old stables have been demolished. To the south of Top Field was a much earlier field with the remains of an old brick kiln. The Teynham Brick Company's field was just east of the Conyer - Greenstreet road, on the turning off the Deerton Street Lane, near Osier Farm. This field was later bought by Eastwoods. To the south, and on the other side of the railway line was Smith's brickworks and nearby a couple of hand berths.

Richardson's also had a cement factory by Conyer Dock, a six-kiln affair on the site of the old oil mill. The oil mill used to be worked by a beam engine and in about 1860, after the mill was converted to a cement works, the engine provided power for the mill and fed power to the brick

Richardson's Cement Mill at Conyer, about 1890. Note the tramway track in the foreground which went all the way to the end of the dock.

fields by means of a cable. The beam from the original engine was erected by the side of Richardson's tramway where it can be seen today.

The other brickfields were situated north of the village down towards the Creek's mouth. These were all owned by Eastwoods. The first to be built was the Butterfly, near the Creek's mouth, from which Butterfly Wharf takes its name. This was in 1885. Butterfly was followed by Klondyke in 1895, which subsided after a few years, and so Conyer Works was built on firmer ground. Conyer Works, opened in 1911, was known as the 'German Works'. It closed in 1965, but brick-making at Conyer strangely enough did not come to an end. Eastwoods (by now Redlands) built a new works just above the Warren in 1972.

In years past people living in Conyer must have been familiar with the process of how bricks are made, but for the reader's benefit they are composed of brickearth (clay) mixed with mud, household

Gangs of workmen dig to fill the tramway hopper wagons with brickearth. The excavation is clearly deeper than the height of the men, probably about eight feet.

Walking the washbacks in 1928, making sure that the liquid mud keeps flowing freely.

Green bricks are made and stacked to dry before they transfer to the cowls (kilns) for firing.

refuse (mainly ash and clinker) with a small quantity of chalk. Eastwoods clay was dug from a field at Lower Newland's, beyond Smiths field, and made into a slurry which was then pumped nearly two miles by underground pipe to the Klondyke. Traces of this pipe can be seen where it crosses dykes on the old course of the Lyn.

The slurry was piped via shutes into washbacks which were enclosed by brick walls. The slurry was left for about a year for the water to evaporate and the residue was covered with a layer of ash, to be dug out and mixed in a pugmill. Green bricks were made from this mixture, stacked on trucks, dried and then stacked by hand in the cowls (kilns) to be burnt. The burning was by coal dust fed into the cowls, but today bricks are burnt in clamps and fired by methane gas.

Fleets of Thames sailing barges were developed to carry the bricks and the cement to London, but this trade had virtually ceased by the start of the last war. A few freights of bricks were taken away post-war and then the Conyer barge trade came to an end.

Blackett's Dock in 1976, silted up almost level with the saltings.

Up to the middle of the last century Conyer Creek was navigable up above Mercer's Wharf (now the limit of navigation) in 3 tributaries: to Blacketts, to Tong Mill which was built on the site of Tong Castle, and with a third tributary to Frognal. An old friend of mine told me that his father could remember the time when barges came away from Tong Mill with corn. The upper channels ceased to be used and a dock was dug on the west bank of the creek below the village with a wharf which served Blacketts.

At that time there was no 'Dock' at Conyer, the water just lapped the edge of the lane. Richardson took over Sidders Wharves and dug the old creekway out into a dock and backfilled to form the quay. He also built a row of cottages. The end house nearest to the Ship Inn was originally a store.

I can remember when it had a notice-board, with regulations regarding the use of the wharf painted on it. There were penalties for such things as leaving loads of muck unattended!

Looking down Conyer Dock, the tramway tracks can be seen running along both sides of the dock. Wagons are alongside the sailing barges. This photograph was taken some time after 1911; as the brickfield chimney seen above the other buildings' chimneys in the background was finished in that year.

Below Richardson's was the Parish Wharf, the barge yard, Lower Conyer Wharf and then the high bank, known as the 'Warren', which led towards Eastwoods' brickworks. It would seem that part of the foreshore in front of the Warren down towards the Creek's mouth was the land owned by John Cresswell the Faversham shipowner, and leased to William Beacon. It was the subject of an entry in the 'Revised Tithe Awards' of 1863, and comprised the foreshore between high and low water marks of:

'3 acres 2 rods 10 perch'.

There is another entry, written in a copper-plate hand, for Giddehorne and Gravel pit fields which amounted to 13 acres, 3 rods, 35 perch, and the tithe was enjoyed by the vicar of Bapchild. Gravel for ballasting the coasters was dug out from the Gravel pits, on the opposite side of the lane to the Warren. Here two Roman burial urns were dug up.

The Revd. George Moore enjoyed the tithe to Lower Conyer Wharf - '14 Perch', and to the Oyster store and Saltings '2 Perch'.

In the same volume I found a reference to the Public House at Conyer. Owned by William Rigden (Brewers) it was tenanted by the aforementioned William Beacon, and the house was then known as the 'Ship Endeavour'. What a lovely name for a waterside Inn; what single

Looking across the dock towards The Ship Inn in the early 1950s. The yacht barge *Saltcote Belle*, not long out of trade and converted by The Whitewall Barge, Yacht & Boat Company at Hoo on the River Medway, is moored in what by this time was a much silted berth.

minded person had shortened it to the 'Ship Inn'? The signboard has had a variety of vessels painted on it over the years. The first I remember was a full rigged ship. Since then, it has had Dutch Barges and Thames Barges, the latter more suited to the Inn's position, but not suited for a Ship. I wonder why it was named the 'Ship Endeavour'? Possibly it was after the Sittingbourne hoy of the same name, which might have traded to the Creek, as the visiting hoys were all Milton Creek owned.

Now the hoys and the brick or cement barges have gone, but a reminder of them remains in the three former sailing barges which are among the houseboats which inhabit what was once the Richardson's Dock. One of them, the Maldon *Mermaid*, was built on the River Blackwater to carry haystacks.

Eastwood's managers and staff gather for a medal presentation. The young man in a blazer to the right of the photograph holds the medal boxes. As in many pictures of Conyer the spars and rigging of sailing barges occupy the background; note also the stack of bricks to the left waiting to be loaded aboard. The date is around 1928.

Chapter 2

Conyer The Day Before Yesterday

I have lived all my life near Conyer Creek and some of my happiest years were those I remember before World War Two, when people had time to sit on the wall and talk about their 'good old days'. Today many people don't have time to sit and talk, some of them don't even have the time to listen.

In my experience most people have interesting subjects on which they can talk, but some need a little persuading to get them started. Yet once started they can talk about many incidents of the past. I hope that by setting down a few of the stories I have been told I may bring back memories to the older residents of Conyer, and to give to those who have come to live here in recent years an idea of the port's past 'for good or for bad'.

To me Conyer is home. Most of my childhood was spent in wandering around the wharves watching the Thames sailing barges load or discharge their cargoes. Although my home was just outside the Conyer limits, at Teynham Street, I was considered a 'Conyerite', which was very different from an ordinary 'Teynhamite'. What the difference was I have never found out, apart from the fact that to me Conyer was the more exciting place in which to spend my time.

The mill stream, where all the children learned to swim, photographed in 1975.

Boats and barges were a fascination to me then as they are to this day. As children we enjoyed the raw healthy life which comes naturally to country bred kids: more often than not we had the backsides out of our trousers, worn torn coats (if you had one) and boots that let the water in one side and out the other (much preferred to those that kept the water in). Nobody seemed to feel the cold. In fact we all learned to swim in the 'Milly' as we called the cold fresh water stream. Having learned to swim there, one was then allowed to swim in the Creek; some swam from the Parish Wharf in front of the Ship Inn, others from the sandy beach at the Warren. In fact you could swim from almost anywhere when the tide was up in the days before World War Two, before the waterfront became enclosed. True, the raw sewage from the houses flowed into the creek at various places, and could be seen floating on the water. If encountered it was brushed aside. I have no recollections of it doing any harm to anyone.

Griping for 'Flatties'.

There was very little money about, so if one wanted a copper or two, one went 'griping' for flatties, a kind of flat fish that used to abound in the creek. These provided the one meal you could get free, and a good meal they made if you were hungry.

The method used to catch them was this: first you waited for low water, then you put on an old pair of shoes or boots, an old pair of trousers and tied a sack around your waist to put the caught fish in. Then you entered the channel at Mercer's Wharf; walking side by side across the channel, working with the tide so that the muddy water flowed in front of you. To 'gripe' for flatties you placed the hands close together and bent over until your chest touched the water. With fingers spread you pressed your hands into the mud, covering the area in front of you, working your way along until you felt your first fish. Usually the first one got away as it wiggled, causing you to ease the pressure in surprise. When you feel your fish the thing to do is to press it into the mud, then wrap your fingers under it so that you can lift it out to place it in the sack tied around your waist; this sack hung in the water to keep the fish alive. The reason you work with the flow of the water is to stir up the mud so that the fish cannot see you coming, otherwise they dart off, leaving a trail of 'smoke' where they stir the bottom with their tails. If they cannot see you they lie still, very seldom moving. Many is the time I have seen people pop into the Creek, grap a

'Caught one.'

couple of flatties for their tea, and set off home with them.

There used to be an abundance of shell fish along the Swale, and nearly every house had its garden path made up of empty shells - winkles, mussels and whelks were there for the taking. Pollution has put an end to the shell fish of the Swale Creeks. This is the price society pays for the march of progress! How many years before we pollute this world of ours so that there is nothing left for us to feed the millions of hungry mouths? It frightens me to think about it.

In my childhood days we used to be as at home roaming the marshes as we were by the creekside.

We knew where all the wild birds' nests were and visited them daily, waiting for the young to hatch, then watching the parents feed them. In time we saw the fledgelings leave their nest, saw the mothers encouraging them to use their wings, until all at once they were gone. But there was so much to see! We could sit on the sea wall of the Swale and watch the porpoises hunting for fish, their gracefully curved backs leaving the water; always shining with wetness, they would look like children at play - fascinating to watch. Again, pollution drove their food away. Perhaps, they will come back when pollution has been reduced to a bearable level.

The 32 ton sailing barge *Landrail* seen hulked at Butterfly Wharf by the mouth of Conyer Creek in 1953. She was built by Letley at Lower Halstow for Eastwoods in 1894, staying in their ownership all her life, the last few years as a mud lighter for brick-making.

We also wandered down to the bank of the Swale, past Butterfly Wharf to the Creek's Mouth. Although most of the paths and walkways around Conyer have been lost to the public for various reasons, one can still walk, as we used to, from Conyer to Oare along the seawall. The red-sailed oystersmacks or barges are rarely seen now, except for a few privately owned ones which still sail these

waters, but nature has not altered and this walk is still well worth the effort. It takes you through the longest unspoilt stretch of coastline in the south east and has been included in a conservation area.

Over many years I have collected information, stories, yarns (not always true or printable) about Conyer and its people. At the same time I have watched its industries die a slow but inevitable death. The only industry which has returned is brickmaking, after a short slumber.

Fishing was one of the first of the local industries to die. Its demise was caused by the building of larger fishing vessels at places like Whitstable and Ramsgate. These vessels caught greater amounts which had to be sold away from their home ports, and this meant a reduction in price, thereby making it impossible for the small boats to compete. The Oyster trade in the Swale went in the same way but the cause was pollution; the Faversham Oyster Company must have once had the lion's share of the market locally.

The closure of the Cement Mills and of the Co-operative and the Mercer's Brickfields caused a rapid decrease in the barge trade in Conyer. The building of small motor coasters slowly put an end to the building of sailing barges, although the barges sailed on for many years they gradually became fewer and fewer. After the Second World War only a mere handful was left trading, compared with the numbers working before the First World War.

I started my working life in one of Conyer's dying industries, that of barge building. There were still plenty of barges to be repaired, but what wooden barges there were to be built were much sought after by other yards who, like ourselves, were looking for work. This made building very competitive. I am sure we were often building craft at a loss, making what profit we could on the repair side, little though that was.

It was a feeling for Conyer, where I had spent so many happy years, that prompted me to write about it and its people. But where to start was a problem. It was reading Betty Klitgaard's book 'Sailing Troubadour' that decided me.

A barge framed up with the wale cramped in position c.1934. I wonder if one could obtain an oak plank as long and as knot free as this today. The plank must be between 35 and 40 feet long, 15 inches wide and three and a half inches thick. The timber frames can be seen dovetailed into the floors with a naval plate on every fifth timber. Only best quality oak was used; the surveyor used to inspect each stage of building, making it impossible to use inferior timber.

The Klitgaards had a boat at Conyer about 1934. Klitgaard was an operatic singer and his wife a dancer. Work in those fields was hard to get so they came to live on their boat, almost in poverty, living from day to day. Many people still remember his lovely voice when he gave impromptu concerts in the club room of the Ship Inn.

Eventually they left Conyer, and it was Betty Klitgaard's parting words that gave me a start to this book. About the people of Conyer she says: 'During our stay we had made many friends among these kind neighbourly villagers. There was the old lady who sent her little girl regularly every Sunday morning with a bunch of Asters; from another family came baskets of beans and carrots grown in their tiny allotments; yet another of these generous people would ask if we'd care to try 'just a few' of his potatoes and leave half a sackful. Simple, open hearted souls because they knew that times were hard, and because they too knew the meaning of poverty.'

So I will start with people, after all it is the people that make village life and it is life that makes the village.

Once commercial craft ceased to use the dock, many vessels arrived for use as houseboats. This 1969 picture showing three ex-working craft, the barges *Gold Belt*, and at the top of the dock, *Persevere* as well as the ketch *Isabel*. Ahead of *Isabel* lies a wartime ML, and to the left a much smaller boat, but still somebody's home, with its dockside garden well tended.

Chapter 3

Some People of Interesting Character

The Ship Inn is the backdrop for the two shipwrights working on the fit out of the motor yacht *Sundowner*, built here for a Commander Lightoller by Charlie Cooper. Note that the 'gangplank' is an old barge hatch cover.

At one time Conyer was full of people who could be described as 'characters'; many come to mind, and to write about them all would fill volumes.

There were quite a few large families living at Conyer in the nineteen-thirties, and as in most large families there is sure to be at least one real 'character', and when a family gathered at home all sorts of happenings might, and invariably did occur.

When two such characters got together the potential for excitement multiplied, whether planned or on the spur of the moment, but happen it did.

Going back to just after World War Two, Boxing Day if my memory is right, the members of the Manser Family were all assembled in the Ship Inn at mid-day, something they had done for years. Also at the Ship was Bert Webb. In fact the Inn was full of locals, not unusual for a Boxing Day, as in those days all the Conyer people came home for the family reunion at Christmas.

Now as it happens on this particular Boxing Day, when all at the Ship Inn were trying hard to sober up from the previous day's celebrations, who should appear but none other than the same rag and bone man that called the previous year, and probably the year before that, getting in first to purchase rabbit skins which were always in abundance at that time of the year. Most people had rabbit with their Christmas dinner as a second meat to help out with the turkey. Arriving at the front of the Ship Inn he started his rounds of the cottages to buy his rabbit skins. No sooner out of sight than one of the Manser boys and Bert Webb mounted the rag and bone man's cart and in a very short time were giving rides to all through the village and back. Tiring of this they next took the horse out of the cart and with the seasonal feeling of goodwill to all men and horses, they took the horse into the bar where they gave him a pail of beer to drink, which to everyone's surprise, the horse did.

By now every one present had joined in the spirit of the thing, so that when an irate rag and bone man came back in to the pub demanding to know what was going on, he was propelled to the bar protesting, where he was plied with pint after pint of beer, many of which had been laced with the odd whisky, or two.

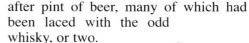

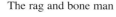
The rag and bone man

After some time of this unexpected and over generous treatment, unable to stand without assistance, and not knowing what he had come into the bar for, he was carried out to his cart and secured to his seat.

During the time he was in the bar with these hospitable, generous and friendly natives, someone had harnessed his horse to the cart back to front. One had to imagine what happened when they handed him the reins, but they had had their fun and soon put things right. Perhaps it was the best Boxing Day he had enjoyed for many years.

The bar returned to its proper use, but only for a short time. It was packed to capacity with hardly room to put your hand in your pocket to buy a round of drinks, when all of a sudden it was full of flying, cackling, screaming chicken, which had been fetched from the landlord's hen house and thrown through the bar's rear entrance. Feathers were flying everywhere, getting up noses, down throats and into beer glasses. I can't see this sort of thing happening today, or could it?

This was the normal run of village life around that period of time. The men worked hard for little pay, most of them worked in the brickfields under conditions that turned young boys into old men in a very short time; can one wonder at them enjoying themselves when the opportunity arose?

Apart from the occasional sprees, the people of Conyer were a sober lot. The majority of them attended church on Sundays, whole families walking to church together.

Family life at Conyer was clearly one of togetherness. On hot days whole families could be seen swimming together, some from the wharf in front of the Ship Inn, others off the sandy beach at the Warren, where once there was a footpath which had been in use as long as any of the old inhabitants could remember. This has now disappeared under a modern marina.

Feathers were flying

All those access points have unsightly prison-like fences surrounding them now, something that was never needed, and to my way of thinking is still not needed. I visit a lot of waterside villages each year when out sailing, but nowhere have I seen one with so little access to the water for the general public.

The inhabitants of Conyer were, in fact, very honest. I remember at the beginning of World War Two when Captain Tom Garn, who lived on his cabin cruiser moored opposite the Ship Inn, was called up for service. He had a large pile of coal on the wharf. On his return after the war he found the coal pile still intact, in spite of coal shortages throughout the war years.

In all the time that I worked at the shipyard I cannot remember the sheds or our tool boxes being locked, nor can I remember anything being missing, even though people could walk in as they pleased. It was quite normal for people to wander in to see what progress had been made when we were barge building. One daughter of a Conyer barge captain told me that as a girl it was her job to find kindling wood for their fires; this would be collected along the Warren, washed up by the tide. On one of her trips near the shipyard she noticed a short end cut off a plank, which she picked up. On arriving home with her load her father noticed the short end of plank; he asked her where she had picked it up, and on being told near the shipyard, she was ordered by her father to return it the exact place where she had found it. He said it was stealing to pick up anything on private property.

There were rogues, of course, but they made sure not to steal in their own community. Circumstances made them rogues in order to survive. There were no hand outs by the State as there are today, which as we know, are openly abused by some.

Life could be hard in winter. A bleak, frozen and snowy Conyer dock in 1938/9. On the left of the picture can be seen two of the tramway trucks that carried the bricks from the Teynham Brickfield to be loaded into the sailing barges.

One particular old local I used to spend many hours talking to was George Mills or, as he was locally known, 'Darkie'. He must have been well over ninety when he passed away. He lived in the armoury at the rear of Coastguard Cottages for many years.

I first met 'Darkie' when I worked at the shipyard. His brother, who was much older, was known as 'Trimmer'. He was a tall lean man, whereas 'Darkie' was shorter and thick set. The two of them would sit on a stack of planks outside our sheds, 'Trimmer' would be wearing a woolly be-tasselled hat, the tassel hanging down one side of his face, his hands clasped together over the top of a well worn walking stick which was placed between his feet, and a pipe (which never seemed to be alight) in one side of his mouth. On warm days his head would gradually sink onto his clasped hands and he would doze off, his closed eyes now pointing to his boots whose laces never seemed to be tied up.

'Trimmer' and 'Darkie'

'Darkie', who always wore a black cap would sit with one elbow resting on his knee, his hand holding the pipe that was always in his mouth from which belched clouds of smoke curling away upwards in the warm summer air.

Very few words would be spoken between the two brothers unless a barge topsail could be seen over the warren bank as it made its way up the twisting creek to Conyer. Then the two brothers would start an argument as to which barge it could be. 'Trimmer' was nearly always right, 'Darkie' would argue for the want of something better to do, or to try and make 'Trimmer' swear.

During one of my long talks with 'Darkie' he related to me the story of a barge captain who went into the Ship Inn, ordered a meal and was duly served with it at one of the bar tables. On commencing his meal the landlord's cat took up station on the opposite side of the plate and joined the captain in his meal. The captain allowed this to continue for some time, then he was heard to say 'I don't mind you having a bite but you are eating faster than I'. With this he lifts the cat's tail and dabs a spoonful of mustard under it. The next few minutes were pandemonium as the cat took off like a rocket around the bar knocking bottles and glasses flying everywhere.

One can imagine a bar full of customers (some of them already over imbibed), trying to escape the frantic actions of this poor creature, their own behaviour only adding to the chaos.

Many years ago I checked this story with two old customers at the Ship Inn and they both confirmed it, one even named the barge captain involved.

'Darkie' and 'Trimmer' had a bawley boat moored at the wharf close to the Ship Inn. The wharf was then considered a public wharf, where all moorings were free until after the Second World war. The brothers would not move their bawley boat for anyone, although it lay alongside Richardson's wharf it was not moored to it, being moored aft to the public wharf with an anchor out forward. It was explained to me by a barge captain that when Richardsons built the dock they took the wharf to their extreme limits so that anyone could lay there as long as they did not make fast to the wharf. Whether this is true, I have never found out.

Around 1935 there was a shortage of work, so 'Darkie' took on anything that came along as long as it suited him. He was tremendously strong for his age, and thought nothing of breaking up old barges just for the wood to burn in his one room home. Breaking up any old vessel is just about the hardest work anyone could wish to do.

I was sad to see the passing of this grand old man who would push his punt down down the channel and work his way out of the creek to do a bit of fishing on frosty mornings.

'Darkie' once told me that he was called up for the army during the First World War; this was not quite to his liking, and he decided it was not the life for him. He told me that one day he was late for a meal. It was not his fault, but something to do with a particular drill that he had to learn correctly before he was dismissed. On eventually arriving at the table he noticed that someone had 'swiped' his meat from off his plate, leaving only potatoes. Picking up his plate he said, 'The one that has had my meat can have my spuds', with that he emptied it over the head of the man he suspected of taking it.

He got, as he said, 'Jankers' for that and from then on he was a marked man. Nothing went right for him, so he made up his mind to get out of the army. He became untrainable and broke his Sergeant Major's heart, if that were possible. Eventually they discharged him. He would give a soft chuckle and say that he was the only man the army could not train.

Before the First World War 'Darkie' had found employment at the shipyard helping Harry French to collect timber from either the Railway Station, or the steam saw-mills which were close to the station; they collected this on a timber tug pulled by two horses.

This arrangement lasted for some time, but as 'Darkie' told me, 'It was a thirsty job.' and frequent stops at the Railway Tavern and the Brunswick Arms on the short journey to the shipyard caused delays, which put a sudden stop to the arrangement.

After this job ended 'Darkie' drifted from job to job, with a bit of fishing in between. Even when fishing 'Darkie' managed to get into awkward situations. A relative of 'Darkie' told me of the time when he and his brother 'Trimmer' were sailing their bawley boat to the fishing grounds; the wind was light, the day warm, the water in the Swale looked inviting, so 'Darkie' decided to go for a swim. Stripping off all his clothes he dived overboard as naked as the day he was born. After a considerable time in the water he looked for the boat which was getting further and further away. The wind had increased during the time 'Darkie' had been in the water. 'Heave to' he shouted to his brother, but 'Trimmer' had no such intentions. 'You wanted a swim, now you can swim home'. 'Darkie's' clothes were still on board the boat!

'Darkie' had a wonderful sense of humour, he spoke with a deep soft voice, and his soft chuckles were very infectious. After visiting his brother, who was not able to get out very often in his old age, he met Peter Parrish. 'What do you think, Peter, I have just been to see 'Trimmer', and he was sitting in his chair with his feet in the oven. Said they were cold'.

'Trimmer' warms his feet.

During the time that I worked at the shipyard 'Darkie' came to break up the old coasting barge *Nonpariel* together with a First World War Motor Launch (M.L.). This had been bought by the White family who owned the shipyard, for sentimental reasons; a relative had served on it during the war. The vessel had lain there for over twenty years. All the local people used it for a changing room when they went swimming; the owners turned a blind eye to this, knowing that they would never abuse the use of this facility. Whether one could assume the same today - who knows?

The M.L. was in very good condition considering her age, her grey wartime paint was still intact over most parts. 'Darkie' sold a lot of the timber which he salvaged from her. I used to watch him carrying large sections upon his back, and marvelled at his strength for one so old.

As the years passed by 'Darkie' took longer to walk to the Ship Inn for his Sunday lunchtime pint. In the end he would have to sit on the washback wall to rest and light his pipe; a pint would always be on the counter waiting for him as soon as he stepped into the bar.

'Darkie' was very popular with the customers and most of them treated their old friend; he was, in fact, very independent and did not take kindly to being treated too often. He had sat on a seat in a corner for years and that seat was kept vacant for him. If a stranger was sitting in it someone would politely ask him to move. Many's the time I have seen a tear come to the old boy's eyes as my father quietly slipped him an ounce of tobacco.

At Christmas there would be a whip-round for 'Darkie'. On receiving it, not being able to find words, he would just nod his head to all in the bar (which was understood by them), happy that they had made his Christmas a bit more cheerful. Towards the end of 'Darkie's' life there was so much he wanted to tell me but he just could not talk for long at the time. I then realised that I was about to lose a link with the past, a grand old link at that.

In a little bungalow opposite the Ship Inn, once lived Mrs. Terry and Tom, her husband. Mrs. Terry, an immaculately clean woman of very tidy appearance, she was a little plump, but perhaps this was an impression given by her shortness of stature. Her voice was deep but pleasant to listen to. There was always a 'good morning' or whatever time of day it happened to be. A busy little woman, she always gave one the feeling that she had two days' work to do and only one day to do it in. She took in washing for a living, mostly from the better off type of people who could afford what would be termed a luxury in those days. Her washing would put to shame a lot of washing that comes from the modern washing machines of today, which, in spite of the millions spent on advertising 'whiter than white', seem to get greyer than grey.

Her little home was as spotless as her washing, and one could see on entering that she was very proud of her house. Her brass curtain rails looked as bright as a button, as though they were polished every day.

Mrs. Terry told me that she had been a dresser in the theatre most of her life, and she had dressed some of the best known stars of her day, and by the way she dressed when going out for the day she must have inherited some of their clothes.

Tom was a sort of mystery. He never seemed to have a permanent job. At times he would go bird trapping, or in season do a bit of bird scaring for a local farmer. I knew he did a little scrap metal dealing, taking his scrap to Chatham to sell to a well known merchant, subsequent to which he and the scrap metal dealer would go across the road to the public house and stay until closing time. Tom would arrive home on the bus much later, and a bit worse off for drink.

To the left of this photograph, taken in 1923, is the Ship Inn. The bungalow to the right was the home of Mrs. Terry. At one time it was a nine-pin bowling alley and had a thatched roof which was replaced later by corrugated iron. Stacks of barge building timber can be seen in front of the Ship Inn. The creek is just out of view to the left.

Occasionally Tom and his wife would wander across to the Ship Inn just for a quick drink. Some time later they would be seen crossing the road to their bungalow supporting each other, both accusing each other of being drunk.

Conyer seemed to have a lot more high tides then than they do now. When these were imminent cart-loads of mud were brought to the village. This was used to seal the doors to stop the sea water from entering the houses, or at least to try and check the main flow.

Not taking any chances the people affected would raise their furniture and floor coverings above the expected tide level. On these occasions Tom would slip across to the Ship Inn and get drunk. The thought of moving the furniture was too much for him. When this happened Mrs. Terry would come across to the shipyard and ask Mr. Gates if she could borrow me to help her raise her furniture. Mrs. Terry was always in command of herself on these occasions and knew just where to move the furniture to and which needed moving.

Many times I have collected Tom from the Ship Inn and put him to bed all standing, for which I was rewarded with a packet of cigarettes - 'paid for with money from Tom's pocket' Mrs. Terry used to say to me as she gave them to me the next morning.

Mrs. Terry.

Some time after World War Two a form of benefit became available to married pensioners, and it was no little surprise to me when I was asked to go into the Ship Inn and have a drink with Mr. and Mrs. Terry who had that day been to the registrars office and got themselves married. The bride looked resplendent, her hat lavished with feathers.

The Terry's have long since gone, and so has their little bungalow, which must originally have been one of the old fisherman's cottages, later to become a nine-pin bowling alley mainly for the use of the coastguards stationed at Conyer. The modern houses that occupy the site now, of pseudo 'Georgian' design, will never replace the charm and humble dignity of their little cottage.

Outside the Brunswick Arms around 1888. Mr. French was landlord, and he also had his 'carrier' business which carted timber for the barge yard. He also ran the Conyer horse bus which took people to 'town' once a week, giving them 3 hours shopping before the return journey. The family seen on board are the Harveys, who were related to French, the baby Doris Harvey.

'Straights' Millen would have made an ideal subject for a cartoonist, not very tall, wiry looking, bent legs which needed the aid of a stick to help them along. Cap worn on the side of his head, it was remarkable how this combination of legs and stick propelled him along at a fair lick, especially in the direction of the Brunswick Arms, or the Ship Inn.

Having been bought up on 'Nelson's Blood', the occasional urge to remind him of its taste led him in the direction of the two above named. As he liked to visit both houses, the Brunswick Arms being the nearest by far, he would call in there first to energise himself for the second half of his journey.

Although I have never seen the time when 'Straights' could not get back home under his own power, I am reasonably sure there must have been the odd occasion. It was one of these visits that finally did for this remarkable old sailor. Coming out of the Ship Inn he tripped on the concrete forecourt and injured himself. He never recovered, but apparently passed away peacefully.

He lived with his brother at Stone Chimney. Both were bachelors as far as I know. 'Straights' was retired and stayed at home doing the cooking and the housework. He had been a Royal Navy sailor, and like all of that breed, he was spotlessly clean and tidy. I spent many hours in his house listening to his yarns on life aboard ships in his day.

He had joined the Royal Navy at an early age in the transitional period when some of the ships still carried yards crossing their masts. The washing down of decks was done in bare feet, trousers rolled up at the bottom to just below the knee. He told me that he used to draw so much blue serge and so much white duck from ships stores and make his own clothes. He gave me two white fronts which he had

'Straights' Millen.

made many years previously, all hand sewn and beautifully finished. With the passing of 'Straights', another of my connections with the past had been severed; in spite of the age difference I missed the company of this old Sea Dog.

The only former bargeman still living in Conyer today is Ted Beacon, who had served either as mate or captain on the sailing barges *Oak, Frognal, Warwick, Durham, Northampton, Clare, Surprise, Dabchick* and the little *Band of Hope*. Ted had worked under various owners, finishing his barging days with Eastwoods. His father had been captain of Richardson's barges many years ago.

Captain Ted Beacon, the last of the Conyer bargemen living in the village, pictured in 1973.

There had been three full-time Skippers living in Conyer up to the Second World War; Eli Head, Alf Whitehead, and Fred Harris. Eli Head had retired from regular barging but did a lot of huffling - which was piloting vessels in and out of the creek. He eventually got round to pressing me into helping him. The work mostly consisted of taking out a loaded barge from the dock and anchoring it in South Deep, so that its regular skipper could pick it up at his leisure. Sometimes it meant sailing a barge in. We would go down to the seawall by South Deep on our bicycles. These we would put in the barge's boat which would be anchored close to the shore where the skipper left it, then we would row off to the barge, set the topsail and then raise the anchor. With a bit of luck we could sail most

The dock around the 1930s. Captain Eli Head rows a barge's boat down the dock. Mrs. King's shop is seen with the white fence around it; the lorry to the left belonged to Crafter and Cheeseman. The roof of the building seen to the right of the shop is that of the shed where Charlie Cooper built boats. The brickworks' chimney can just be seen in the left background.

of the way in. At other times we would have to use the setting booms (long poles) most of the way; this was when you earned your money! Eli was paid two and sixpence, of which he gave me tenpence. I have often thought what a lot of responsibility it was on a man for so little reward. I have since found out that the pay had been two and sixpence since long before the First World War; inflation was not known then.

I recall once that we picked up a barge at South Deep and were tacking her up towards the Creek entrance. The army was using the rifle range near the shore at the time - they displayed a red flag each side of the targets, with a man attendant to signal the officer in command when a vessel was entering the firing area. As we were already in the area we raised our anchor, the signal had already been given. We were for some reason delayed in making a start which brought the young officer on to the sea wall to see what was holding up his shooting. There was a good tide that particular day and we had a head wind making it necessary to tack; one of our tacks headed us towards the young officer, now surrounded by a number of N.C.O.s and other ranks. We knew that we had plenty of water under our bottom right up close to the sea wall, so we took advantage of this and were really charging headlong towards the group standing on the wall. When we were within three lengths of the wall the young officer, not knowing that a barge can come about in so short a space, was heard to shout 'He has lost control of the barge', and with this they all disappeared down the other side, soon wondering what stroke of luck had prevented the two idiots on the barge from smashing a hole through the sea wall.

All the Conyer skippers had time off to skipper the yacht barges in the summer months. This must have been better than freighting; at least there was no hurry to get to their destinations, no worry over lost tides, or missed freights.

Alf Whitehead's father had been on the barges. In later years he too did huffling. In those days it had to be done on night tides as well,

38

owing to the sheer numbers of barges using the Creek. My Aunt Alice, who was his daughter, told me that one dark and windy night her father left home to go to South Deep to pick up a barge to bring into the dock. Many hours passed and he had not returned, so her mother kept putting her coat on and going out into the black night to see if she could see anything. The night was so black, there were no street lamps in those days, so that she could not see a thing. This caused her great anxiety until finally her husband came home in the early hours.

On being asked why he had been so long, he smiled and told her the tale that all seamen seem to have ready when they are a few hours late, or adrift.

It appears that he went to South Deep and waited for the tide, but one of those inexplicable things happened; no tide came. I have known this happen twice while I worked at the shipyard. On seeing that he would not be able to get the barge in on the tide, he walked home and this meant that he had to pass the Ship Inn. Now it appears that the landlord had got married that day and happened to see him passing. As it was a cold and dirty night, he invited him in to have a drink to warm him up. Apparently the two got to talking and forgot the time. So, many drinks later, and not thinking anyone was worrying about him, he at last went home. My aunt said that what they could not make out was the fact that he did not as a rule drink.

Another I have good cause to remember is the barge master Fred Harris. He would occasionally come and help in the shipyard doing odd jobs. One day he was helping me when all of a sudden he decided he needed a chew of tobacco - they all chewed it at one time as no

The steam crane at the dock unloading coal for the cement mills, about 1900. It was still in its shed in 1969 at the head of the dock, not having worked since 1927. It was cut up in that year. The crane driver was Bob Couchman, Tubman Tom Parrish, Barge Captain Fred Harris. The barge at the entrance to the dock is tiller steered, both barges are stumpy rigged. The crane was later driven by George Harvey Snr.

Capt. Fred Harris about 1918. He was first in Richardson's barges and later with Eastwoods.

smoking was allowed in the yard. He took a prick of tobacco out and cut off a piece; it looked good enough to eat and like a fool I told him so. He then asked me to try a piece, and thinking I was man enough to chew, I agreed. He cut me off a piece and told me to just chew and chew until I had a mouthful of spit, not to swallow any of it but to spit it out when my mouth was too full, otherwise it would dribble out of the side of my mouth and make a brown stain which could not be tolerated by good chewers. This I did although I confess to not liking it very much. Perhaps it gets better as you go on I thought. Fred had laid his road in well; this innocent youth was working on his third mouthful and thinking which side of this mouth he would professionally spit out of when his teacher gave a hearty slap on the back. I swallowed the lot. No need to say here how sick I was! After I came back from Hell, I looked at Fred expecting to see him laughing at my misfortune, but no, I have never seen him look so serious. He looked me straight in the eye and said 'I have just cured you of one the filthiest habits, and I wished I had never started myself; one of these days you will thank me for it'. How true were his words!

Ben Lewis was foreman shipwright for Alf White for a good many years. Apparently he was a force to be reckoned with and had full control of all hands working in the sheds. They were a rough lot, and the very nature of their work made them tough hard workers and heavy drinkers; tobacco chewers and swearers, with the occasional one or two more pious ones.

They had regular 'fetchins'. This meant taking a three gallon pail to the Ship Inn and having it filled with beer, which went on all day. George Gates did tell me of one lad who dared put his lips to the pail while still in the backyard of the pub. He had made sure to shut the gate on his way in, thereby thinking no one could see him. But one of the shipwrights working high on the stem of a

Ben Lewis, master shipwright. Photograph taken in the late 1920s.

barge happened to look out of the shutter at the end of the shed which overlooked the pub's backyard and caught him in the act of swigging; this was never allowed. They waited until he had put the pail down and then gave him a good box round the ears. My Aunt Alice told me that children were afraid of Ben as he used to shout at them to clear off. This I am sure was done to keep them from hearing the foul language that was used in the sheds. The language was so bad that a path behind the row of houses was made by women taking their husbands meals to the brickfields, so that they could avoid passing the sheds.

Ben had the misfortune to lose the use of one arm which caused him to retire early. Walter Lewis, who still lives at Stone Chimney, the same house that his grandfather Ben had lived in, told me that his grandfather, when examined was found to have an extra rib on the side where the arm lost its use; continual use of maul and adze had caused severe wear to a leader which the extra rib had rested on.

Ben had a smallholding at the back of his house where he reared pigs and grew fruit; this kept him busy and almost every night he would wait for me to come home from work and we would discuss the art of barge building. He would tell me of the days when they were really busy, when all the sheds were full, and as soon as one barge was launched the next day the keel of another was laid.

He was a breed of man that is fast disappearing, a master craftsman. The smell of oak shavings and pine sawdust blended with Stockholm tar had been his life. How he must have craved it in his retirement! He once told me that when the wind was in the right direction he could smell our tar coppers.

Peter Parrish. A picture taken in 1972 when he was 82 years old. One of Conyer's retired brickies.

While chatting to Peter Parrish one night, he told me that his mother had worked in the brickfields. She had been 'Off Bearing' for Harry French who later took the Brunswick Arms. This was a tough job even for a man. But the women were made of tougher stuff in those days simply because they had to do a job to make ends meet. As transport was practically non-existent, it had to be a local job. Peter could remember when the fishing boats unloaded at the Parish Wharf in front of the Ship Inn and one could buy as many sprats as one wanted for twopence. The boats used to bring in sprats, 'five fingers' and mussels which were sold to the local farmers to spread over their land; the 'five fingers' were a menace to the oyster beds and would eat their way through them if not collected and taken ashore.

The wharf and Richardson's Dock were built during this time. Previously the water used to come up the road's edge. The village pump, which everyone had to use, was just on the wharf; (Colonel and Mrs. Blackden have still retained it,

The village pump in 1975. It was the only source of fresh water in the village before piped water was laid, apart from the streams. The pump did not pump water from a well owing to it nearness to salt water.

which I am glad to see). Apparently when some of the locals went to fetch their water, they always took two pails; one for water and one for coal, which lay around in huge lumps. This pilfering got so bad that the Cement Company had the coal lumps whitewashed so that they could see if any were taken; needless to say they still kept disappearing!

Richardson's needed lots of fresh water for their boilers, and as they had a good well at the Teynham brickfield it was decided to use that. A pump was installed at the well and connected to a cast iron pipeline which followed the tramway to Conyer. At the top of the tramroad a tank was built below ground with a pump to raise water for their locomotive, another tank was built at the head of the dock for the use of the steam crane, yet another across the road at the cement mill for its boiler, and another where the pump stands now in the village. All these tanks were connected to the cast iron pipeline, and all were fed from the Teynham brickfield well.

There was once a well which supplied the Ship Inn. This was built over when Richardson built the row of houses opposite the inn, and as far as I know it is still there just inside one of the cottages' rear entrance.

A lot of barges used to use the Creek then, so some of the barge skippers came ashore and did huffling. Some names Peter recalled were J. Spice, Mr. Whitehead and 'Bear-Up' Cooper. Many of the barges using the Creek belonged to Lee & Eastwood, black-sailed, with a white flying horse on the sails. A few of these were 'swimmies' which, if there was a 'plop' on, could be heard coming a long way off, the noise being made by the water slapping up under their swimheads.

Talk about beer drinkers! No one drinks beer today like they used to. The landlord would push a barrow load of beer to the cement mills more than once a day and the landlord of the Railway Tavern did the same up to the Top Field. The men used to sweat it out as fast as they drank it. One foreman Peter remembered used to send a boy to the Inn for a quart bottle which he used to lay in the long grass to keep cool. But his mates would watch where he put it and when his back was turned, help themselves.

Martha Head pictured at about the time she served as mate on her husband's barge.

On the 17th. March, 1975, I visited Martha Head, widow of Eli Head, then in her 91st year, a wonderful lady for her age, remarkably alert and talkative. She did all the talking, as she said 'Glad to have someone to talk to'. Her eyesight was also excellent, in fact she still reads without glasses, but admits to not being able to run about now. She was a descendant of the Beacons, born Martha Harris, sister to Fred Harris, one of Conyer's barge skippers. Another brother was Jack Harris, shipwright. Her sister married Leslie Cheeseman who, with his partner Cecil Crafter, ran a haulage business from the wharf. Leslie Cheeseman later left the partnership to start the filling station at Norton crossroads.

Martha told me that the Ship Inn had been in her family for almost a hundred years, starting with the Beacons, then the Frosts, followed by the Mitsons and finally the Trices. Tom Trice had worked in the Cement mill and when Mrs. Mitson lost her husband she carried on the pub. Tom, who was a regular customer, got to wooing her over his pints. His workmates at the mill were quick to notice this and used to chant a little verse when ever they thought Tom was within hearing - it went like this:

> Tommy, Tommy, Tommy,
> Now's the time to marry,
> With a nice little widow,
> And a nice little pub;
> Plenty of baccy and beer,
> And plenty of grub.
> We will come round to see you
> And keep you company
> Wouldn't it be nice for her
> And wouldn't it be nice for me.

I was amazed at the way Martha quoted these lines so quickly after so many years.

The Ship Inn in those days was a Rigden house, later to become George Beer and Rigden. Martha enjoyed her life at the pub. Beer was twopence a pint. Gin, Whisky and Brandy threepence a half quartern; Rum was fourpence, but the customers wanted hot water and sugar supplied with it free, also a spoon to stir it with!

Meals were served in the bars in those days, and they sold bacon over the counter. Most people who had meals there were barge crews and they enjoyed a bit of fun with their meal. On one occasion the sweep was at the pub sweeping in the bar chimney. His name was Post and he had a hand barrow which he had to push from Greenstreet. His

Lower Road, Conyer about 1925. The Ship Inn can be seen at the end of the road. Jutting out in front of the Inn on the right can be seen Mrs. Terry's bungalow. The wooden house on the right originally stood at the end of Richardson's dock. It was lived in by a Mr. Blake who was the manager of the cement mill. He later had built the house adjoining the cement mill. After he moved into the new house, the wooden house was cut in half and moved to its site shown in the photograph. It is thought that the Windmill owned by the Sidders brothers stood near this site, further up the bank. Nearest the camera can be seen the walls of the washbacks where the slurry was stored for the cement mill.

was thirsty work. Post had a few drinks before he started and after he finished a few more. Then the customers took over, plying him with drink after drink until he was drunk. Then they washed half of his face and whitewashed it. They sat him in his barrow and pushed him to the bottom of the Brum Hill where they convinced him that he was a black and white minstrel, leaving him singing at the top of his voice and trying to push his barrow up the hill.

At this point of my talk with Martha I wished that I had learned the art of shorthand, or had a tape recorder with me. I was finding it difficult to keep up with her and my writing was getting worse, so much so that I was frightened that it would be unreadable. I was afraid to stop her as it was obvious to me that she was enjoying every minute of it.

We had then got back to the Beacon family. One of her relations was Bill Beacon, a barge captain who was killed when the mast of his barge fell on him. Then there was 'Bissel', George, 'Snip', Alf and Ted, all employed by the cement company. Most of them worked on the barges at some time or other and all lived at lower Conyer in Richardson's houses which they rented at four shillings a week until Mr. Richardson died. They then came under Richardson of Vauxhall Wharf, London.

Some of the barge captains she remembered were Captain Lewis who was in the barge *Glendower*; Captain Ernie Shrubshall had one of Richardson's barges; Captain Wraight took a new barge off the ways which had been built by Whites for Darens the millers, 'They had great banners flying in Conyer advertising Daren bread on the day she was launched.' She also remembered Captain 'Bear-Up' Cooper

Afloat at Conyer Dock, Captain 'Bear-Up' Cooper, about 1910.

who at one time was in barges. his wife sailed with him as mate; she was a woman of ample proportions and had great difficulty getting through the cabin hatches. Martha produced a photograph of 'Bear-Up' which was taken on the wharf facing the Ship Inn.

Martha told me that during the First World War Eli Head's mate was called up in the services along with many more barge mates. Some of the Captains sailed their barges single handed, but Eli decided to take his wife along as mate. At the time he was in a barge belonging to the London & Rochester Trading Company named *Sir Richard*. In spite of the possible dangers, Martha decided to take the job, all being well with the company. This meant going to Rochester to be interviewed by Mr. Gill, the Managing Director. Mr. Gill put her at ease as soon as they met and agreed to sign her on as mate. I asked her what sort of cargoes they carried, 'Oh, only T.N.T. and mines' she replied. 'We loaded the T.N.T. at the powder works jetty near Faversham Creek in the Swale and took it to Woolwich Arsenal. We weren't allowed any naked lights on board, which meant no hot

The first of the barges built by Lewis A. Glover at Gravesend, the *Sir Richard* was started in April 1899, but was not ready for launching until Thursday 18th. January 1900, when she slid down the ways into the Thames, christened with a bottle of Champagne.

The remains of the Powder Works dock on the Swale in 1976. It was here that Martha Head's barge loaded explosives.

food or drinks; I got fed up with this and smuggled a double burner lamp on board, also a small tin kettle. I used to hold the kettle over the top of the lamp with just enough water in it to make a cup of tea, it took a long time to boil but it was worth it. We always had the red danger flag flying to denote that we were carrying explosives: other craft usually gave way to us. At times I had to take the wheel and the crews of other vessels were surprised to see a woman at the wheel of the explosives barge. The barge was always loaded to capacity and I did not like it when the water came rushing along the deck when the barge heeled over. When carrying mines we had on board one hundred and thirty and never knew where we were to take them until we arrived off Dagenham; most of them would be off-loaded onto other vessels. When carrying T.N.T. to Woolwich it used to annoy me to be searched every time I went ashore to do our shopping, and again when returning to the Arsenal gates.'

Martha was married to Eli in 1911 and as there were so many relatives, nowhere was there a room large enough to accommodate them all. A solution was found in the shipyard: a barge was under construction and the bottom had been laid, so they were allowed to have their wedding breakfast on it. I have never heard of this happening before, but it was a perfect place for barge people to celebrate their wedding.

Martha also used to sail up the London River as she called the Thames, with her brother Fred in the *Jeffie*. Fred's wife also used to sail with him and they used to have to put up with a lot of banter from the dockers. In the later years Eli skippered Colonel Bingham's yacht barge, Martha went along as cook. Although getting on in years they were still together on sailing barges. In fact, they were at Ipswich in 1939 the day war was declared and were told they may have to stay for the duration. But as the Colonel wanted his barge at Conyer, they decided to sail home and left at night under cover of darkness.

This photograph, taken in 1932, shows the work of Charlie Cooper, both afloat and ashore. The white motor yacht moored in the dock is *Sundowner*, built by Charlie Cooper, owned by Cmdr. Lightoller. The white motor yacht being built on the wharf is the *Marner* for Mr. Farmer who was the owner of the little sailing barge *Seagull II*. Capt. Bert Webb left barging to go as skipper of the *Marner* when she was launched. The dutch barge in the floating dock is the *Sirius* owned by Mr. Constantine.

Charlie Cooper senior was the son of 'Bear-Up' Cooper; he was a shipwright by trade, and had worked in White's yard and then started up on his own in a shed at the top of his garden. My late employer, George Gates, told me that after working all day on building barges Charlie would go home at night and build barge boats. In fact he build one in a week of evenings, including working all day Sunday. He must have worked like a Trojan as barge boats were at the minimum fourteen feet long, and all his timber would have had to be cut by hand. He was a very skilled tradesman. Later he moved onto the wharf to build a large yacht for Commander Lightoller. She was a lovely vessel named *Sundowner* and she was built in the open and a slipway was cut through the wharf to launch her.

Commander Lightoller was a survivor of the *Titanic*; about which he wrote a book entitled 'Titanic', published in the U.S.A. for four dollars, but obtainable in this country. He also broadcast his story on the radio. Charles Snr. was taken ill while building on the wharf; he was in fact never to finish the boat he was building. Charles Jnr. completed it after his father's death. Mrs. Charles Cooper told me that when they were putting Charlie into the ambulance he said to his son Charles 'I won't be coming back to Conyer, so goodbye to my boats.' He knew he was dying and never lived to return to his village.

Mrs. Cooper also told me that there had never been more than one son in the Cooper families and it remains so even to this day; her son David has so far only one son, Martin.

Charles Jnr. had no wish for his son David to carry on the business. Mrs.Cooper told me they had seen some pretty hard times, 'Many's the time that my husband has come home and said we have no money to live on because no one paid his bills. Some days we had an egg and a potato each; there were some bad payers about at that time.' (I can vouch for that. My own employer had the same trouble when I worked at the shipyard, and to stop them doing a 'moonlighter' he has sat beside the boat at all hours whilst the tide was in.) The odd one or two gave boat owners a bad name between the wars, and everyone was suspect until proven otherwise.

The notorious 'Lord Haw-Haw' - William Edward Joyce came to Conyer before the Second World War. He lodged with Mrs. Nell Taylor who lived in the row of houses opposite the Ship Inn. He was at first regarded as just another boat owner, which in fact he was. Why he came to Conyer is anybody's guess: the fact that it was off the beaten track may have had something to do with it. His boat was moored at Cooper's yard which was even more remote. Mrs. Cooper told me that her late husband was given the contract to do quite a lot of alterations inside the boat, one job being to cut spaces for water tanks which were, in fact, never fitted.

What sort of a man did William Edward Joyce appear to be at that time. Mrs. Cooper's mother lived next door to Mrs. Taylor and she used to say what a nice gentlemen he was, always polite in every possible way. The same opinion was also held by Mrs. Cooper and her late husband Charles, even after he revealed his true Nazi feelings Charles used to say 'speak as you find', which I am inclined to agree with. This charming manner of Joyce's was obviously a front to his main purpose, though it seems no one penetrated it at the time. It appears that the spaces that Charles cut in the boat to take water tanks were, in fact, spaces for radio transmitters and generators for the sole purpose of transmitting information to Germany. Apparently someone must have been watching Joyce's movements, for when in Dover Harbour his boat was seized and found to contain the transmitters and other equipment which must have been fitted after she left Conyer.

One point Mrs. Cooper made clear to me was that he always paid his bills promptly which, as I know, is more than a lot of blue-blooded so-called Englishmen did.

William Edward Joyce broadcast propaganda all through the war for the German Reich which was pitiful to listen to. At the end of the war he was found wandering in a wood somewhere in Germany; he was brought to trial at Nurenberg, found guilty of treason and sentenced to hang. He was executed by Pierrepoint, the hangman. William Joyce was hanged at London's Wandsworth jail in January, 1946.

Another of Conyer's characters was Tom Garn, ex-army captain, free-lance pilot, world traveller, yarn spinner extraordinary.

I first met Tom when I was still at school. He then lived on a converted Dutch barge which was mysteriously burnt out one night while Tom was visiting friends. Rumours were rife: how did it catch alight? I am reasonably sure that Tom had nothing to do with it. Several arguments point to this: First, he lost everything he owned; all he had was what he stood up in. Secondly, he was a great reader and had a valuable collection of books on board, some of which could not be replaced. Thirdly, I knew he loved that boat and had just spent a lot of time cleaning off and varnishing all the bright woodwork, which to anyone is a labour of love.

Tom was not well liked, he spoke his mind too freely, and most times without thinking; also he had been everywhere, done everything, and knew almost everything, qualities which few people admired.

I put up with Tom's yarns better than most people and gradually gained his confidence, and many hours have I spent in his cosy saloon on board *Sea Miew* drinking tea and yarning. This was when the other side of Tom's life came out; a broken marriage, world wide travel trying to find his Shangri-la, but never succeeding.

I learned a lot about Tom that was not generally known; by just listening - but let's keep to the Tom we know. He was a great friend of Colonel Bingham; they had, I think, served together in the army. Colonel Bingham owned the coasting barges *Bankside* and *Castanet*, and the yacht barge *George* which he lived on through the summer months. The *George* lay along the Warren and Tom's boat was moored alongside, a convenient arrangement as they were friends, but one day it proved to be an embarrassment. Tom, was answering a call of nature, went to the little room only to find that his chemical toilet was full almost to the brim. He had intended to empty it on the outgoing tide but the tide had left, which meant that he would have to carry it over

Tom Garn's Dutch barge *Sea Miew*, on which he lived, became burnt out after a disastrous fire which destroyed most of his belongings. Tom was one of the first boat dwellers; the barge trades had left the docksides a tranquil haven between the two world wars. Two redundant wagons lie on the tramway to the west of the dock.

the mud to the channel. On looking through his hatch he saw that the Colonel's wife and daughter were sitting on the deck of their barge enjoying the afternoon sun. Tom decided this was not the time to empty the toilet, but as the pains grew, the need was greater, so it had to be done, and quickly. Putting on his rubber boots he carefully carried the toilet pail to the edge of the cockpit and balanced it there. Lowering himself over the side he found the pail was level with his head, so decided to carry the pail on his head until he reached the channel. After three or four steps one of his rubber boots refused to leave the mud; this presented quite a problem as he needed both his hands to balance the pail on his head. However, something had to be done, and done quickly, so carefully taking one hand away he slowly lowered it to the top of his rubber boot, then gradually pulling, the boot started to move and came out. This unbalanced him and over slopped the pail spilling all the contents over Tom. Not looking back, Tom struggled free and reached the channel, where he lay down and let the flow of water wash him clean.

Tom came into the shipyard one day and said that he had turned out some books for me and if I liked to call in on my way home they would be ready to collect. This I did, but on going aboard I heard Tom talking to someone, so I did not bother to stop. The next day he came to see why I had not called; he looked a bit puzzled and said that he had not had a visitor all evening. This was the first time I caught him talking to himself. I walked in on many of his one-sided conversations, something that happens to people who live on their own year after year.

Tom had an irresponsible side to his nature. One day we heard shooting (rapid at that) so we all went to see what was going on. Tom was sitting in his cockpit firing a .45 revolver at a tin can floating on the water; someone rang the police who were soon down. Apparently Tom had permission to keep the revolver, so the police told him to go out on the Swale to do his shooting.

This brings me to a story told me by Major Brown, a brother officer of Tom's in World War Two. After the war Colonel Bingham had a motor cruiser at Conyer and Major Brown used to stay on board with him. Talking to him one day, I happened to mention about the revolver incident; he showed no surprise but told me a story that happened during the war. It appears that they were stationed together out in the wilds at some camp or other. During the evening the officers were all summoned to H.Q. They jumped into a Humber staff car and set off along the country lanes. After some time they caught up with a private car which was travelling slowly; this annoyed Tom as the road was too narrow to pass. Tom continued to sound his horn, but to no avail. Suddenly a wider space allowed them to pass and after passing Tom ordered the driver to stop. Thinking Tom was going to give the other driver a ticking off, no one got out. Suddenly there was a shot, then another, four in all; they were rooted to their seats. Fearing Tom had shot the driver they all jumped out, to see the other driver white faced, still alive, but with four flat tyres. Major Brown told me they had a Hell of a job covering up this serious misdemeanor, which cost Tom quite a lot of money.

After the war Tom came back to Conyer where I did some repair work to his *Sea Miew*, which he later sold, buying a large cruiser. He had an advertisement in the local paper offering lessons to budding boating types on boat handling; weekly terms all meals found. The latter they must have enjoyed for Tom was an excellent cook, as I know from experience.

Later Tom bought a house in Boughton, also a new motor cycle to go to and fro on. Most days he would stop and have a chat with me and it became evident to me that Tom was failing in his health. Soon Tom died; I don't think he had any close relatives, just his housekeeper. Tom had a pretty full life serving in two wars and travelling about the world, and I was told he had spent his way through a small fortune when he was a young man.

There were a number of people who chose to live on sailing barges retired from cargo carrying. Some of these folk visited Conyer for a short stay, or to have work done on their craft, but they came to like the peacefulness of the place and decided to stay. Gradually they became integrated with the natives. Most of them employed local labour of one sort or another, such as domestic, gardeners or skippers.

They all joined in the village activities and soon adjusted themselves to the quiet way and pace of Conyer village life. Very soon the weed covered wharves were transformed into beautiful gardens. The family that stayed longest was Commander Crick whose gardens were a joy to see, taking one's eye off the drab buildings of the old cement mills opposite.

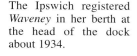

The Ipswich registered *Waveney* in her berth at the head of the dock about 1934.

Waveney, cruising with Capt. Harris at the helm, about 1935, was the home of Commander A. Crick and his family at Conyer. She was owned all her trading life by R. & W. Paul, the Ipswich maltsters. Built for them in 1892, the last of a series named after East Anglian rivers, she was by WWI one of their smallest craft and was the first to be sold for conversion to a yacht in 1933. Just discernable in her topsail is R. & W. Paul's logo, a cross which represented the sails of a windmill. She ended her days derelict at Emsworth, Hampshire where she was burnt in 1964.

Their barge the *Waveney* was moored at the head of Richardson's Dock. On the opposite side of the dock lay the sailing barge *Mermaid*, then the home of Dr. Flint and his wife. We had converted *Mermaid* into a floating home at White's shipyard in the days of G.H. Gates. Other barges which were lived upon and lay in the dock at various times were the *Henry and Jabez*, the home of Major J. Nesham M.C. and his family; *June,* the home of Arthur Bennett,author of the books 'June of Rochester', 'Tide Time' and others and his wife; the *Gold Belt*, home of Colonel Blackden and his wife; the *Pall Mall*, which was owned, I think, by Mr. Bessemer and wife. There were many others that have slipped my memory.

On the other side of the backwater lay the *John and Mary* the home of Squadron Leader D.H. Clarke, another prolific author, his

At the top of the old dock, left to right, are *Gold Belt*, Colonel Bingham's *George* (no spars), *Henry & Jabez*, behind her *Mermaid* (with spars half lowered) and *Waveney* (with topmast aloft). This photograph was taken during the winter months of 1957.

wife Mollie and son Kester. *John and Mary* was also converted at White's Conyer Yard. At the lower wharf at White's shipyard lay the *Glasgow*, home of Mr. Thorpe, his wife and family, again converted at White's yard at Conyer. Along the Warren lay the *Golden Fleece*, home of Mr. and Mrs. Barrus, here also lay the *George*, the summer home of Colonel Bingham and family.

Of the former sailing barges I have mentioned some are still at Conyer to this day. The *Henry and Jabez* is a hulk along the sea wall near Mercer's Wharf, *Mermaid* and *Gold Belt* are still in their old positions in the dock.

Many tough years in trade and, as in the case of *June* of Rochester, a subsequent life as both home and cruising yacht before assuming a static role as a houseboat, took its toll of the structural integrity of the old sailing barges. In the words of the bargemen, they were often 'Tore outs' before becoming homes and eventually hulks in the remote creeks. Here the remains of *June* moulder at Conyer in 1971.

Nine months old, Jeremy Nesham, who did the drawings for this book, surveys the deck from his pram during a family cruise on *Henry & Jabez*.

Immediately after the last war barges went cruising in the summer months with local skippers aboard, some of whom took time off from the brick barges. Freights for them were getting scarce as most of the bricks were being carried by lorries.

Perhaps one of Conyer's most ardent sailors was Dr. Selby. He had a little 20 ft. half-decked sloop which he moored at Charles Cooper's boat yard. On his day off he would go off in her, no matter at what state of the tide, often getting beneaped. He would then sit and wait for the next tide. Other times one would see him, trousers rolled up to his knees pushing her back up the channel with the tide almost gone, and a surgery full of patients awaiting him at home. It was Dr. Selby's wife who wrote the much sought after book 'Teynham Manor and Hundred'.

'Spoilt' and broken bricks were plentiful around Conyer and were put to many uses. Here a bank has been made into a 'rockery' and a play pond built where Jeremy Nesham and David Flint paddle amongst their model boats.

Youngsters living aboard the barges during the 1950s became skilled in the ways of the tidal creeks at a young age. Robert Nesham boards his family's barge *Henry & Jabez* from his wooden dinghy, Debbie Couchman and Jeremy Nesham wait to follow.

Quite often I would meet an old school chum of mine who has a wealth of information on Conyer people. He also has a love of barges and has built many lovely models of them, and he is a gifted painter in water colours. His father worked on the barges and he told me of the time that his father left Conyer in his barge for London.

On reaching Shellness at the end of the Isle of Sheppey the barge's sprit broke in half, a very dangerous thing as this massive spar can do untold damage to anything that happens to be in its path as it falls. The crew was paid by the freight so it was to their benefit to get a new sprit as soon as possible. They found that there was a spare one at Queenborough, provided they collected it themselves. So into the barge's boat they got and rowed to Queenborough, collected the sprit,

Squadron Leader D.H. 'Nobby' Clarke's barge yacht *John and Mary* at Mistley in 1957. 'Nobby' wrote about the barge in his book East Coast Passage.

then rowed all the way back towing the sprit behind their boat. Today no man would do such a thing, or be expected to.

On arriving back to their barge they lowered the mast, somehow managed to sort out the rigging, and prepared to ship the new sprit. On getting it hoisted aboard, a mammoth task for two men, they found it was six feet too long so the head of the sail was temporarily lashed. No doubt the mast had to be lowered when they reached their destination so that the sprit could be fitted properly.

My friend also told me of George Horsenail, a relative of his wife. George had run away to sea when he was young in sailing brigs. Later he came ashore and helped build the barge *Uplees* at Osbourne Dan's Dock on the East Swale. On her completion he shipped in the *Uplees* as mate. Later he was Captain of many different barges, one of them was Burley's *Northdown* which is still afloat as a sailing barge today.

On one occasion when George Horsenail was sailing up Sea Reach in the London River, as the Thames is known to the bargemen, he noticed another barge sailing towards him. There was a strong wind blowing with very heavy gusts. George had intended to pass the other barge to leeward, but just before they met the other barge was knocked down on her beam ends by a particularly powerful gust; there was so much wind pressure in her sails that she would not come back on even keel. It was the quick thinking of George Horsenail which saved the other barge from a certain capsize; he altered his course so that his barge passed the other to windward, and his sails took the wind out of the stricken barge's sails. Relieved of the wind pressure the other barge came back upright.

When Charles Cooper converted the *Haughty Belle* to a barge yacht, George went captain in her, taking her first to Southampton then on to the Continent. This would have been about 1933.

It was only natural that many Conyer youths took to the sea, it was on their doorstep. One well known Conyer character went mate on the brick-barge *Northampton*, whose skipper was know as 'Bones' Wylie. Coming down the London River it came on to blow hard, so 'Bones' decided to anchor under the shelter of the west shore. It happened that the mate was a keen footballer and looked like missing a game if they did not berth by Saturday, so he kept ragging his skipper that he was scared of a blow. The skipper put up with it for some time, then told the mate to set the topsail and break out the anchor. The mate did this willingly, but the voyage home was something that the mater never wanted to repeat, and never again did he accuse his skipper of being frightened of a blow.

Earlier in this chapter Bert Webb was mentioned as one of the pirates of the rag and bone man's cart. Bert had been in sailing barges at one time and had been captain of the brick barges *Coot, Quail* and *Rutland*. His brother 'Fatty' Webb had a spell as mate with him at one time.

My wife and I called on Bert and his wife Violet one evening to spend a couple of hours chatting. It was five hours before we left!

By the time I had started work at the barge yard Bert had left the sailing barges and had gone as skipper on the yacht *Marner*, which was owned by a Mr. Farmer, who had at one time owned the little sailing barge *Seagull II*. I saw a lot of Bert in those days when he came to the yard for paint and other bits and pieces when he was fitting out *Marner*. Bert was skipper of her for a good many years, cruising her from the Solent to the East Coast.

We had a good long chat about Bert's barging days, which like all bargemen at the time, were pretty lean times; sometimes swinging from the buoys for weeks on end without pay. 'Starvation Buoys' they called them, an apt description. At other times it was the other way round, which meant no time ashore between freights. As soon as he was unloaded they loaded him with another cargo, which he could not refuse as he might not have another for weeks.

Bert told me of an instance when this happened to him. He was due to take a load of bricks to London in the *Rutland* on the day after Boxing Day. But subsequently he got orders to sail light on Boxing Day to the Albert Docks to bring back a freight of coal.

Boxing morning was foggy with no wind. When his mate arrived he said that he had a good mind to stay at home. Bert told him it would not have mattered if he had for all the good weather there was. But they set off for South Deep, and by the time they had reached it the wind came up from the south. They were able to get under way and carry their wind right up to the Albert Docks in London.

Eastwood's 'stumpie' barge *Rutland* under sail appears to have a small or light cargo, with plenty of freeboard. Her owner's advertisement was commonplace on the sails of the firm's barges. *Rutland's* mainsail bears an incomplete legend, perhaps the sail was cut down from that of a larger barge. *Rutland* was built in 1900 by Alfred Marconi White at Conyer, but recorded on her registry as built at Teynham.

As soon as they got the hatches off three shutes starting pouring coal in, and in no time at all they were loaded. They then slipped their moorings and carried the ebb down river to the Estuary where they met the first of the flood which carried them up to Conyer. London and back in a day.

On arrival at Conyer Bert met the manager on his way home. Bert asked him if he had got his loading ticket. The manager replied 'Give the bloody postman time to get here'. He told Bert that he was going to get him unloaded and load him up with a cargo of bricks to go away on the evening tide. Bert was still covered with coal dust and had not had any sleep. When he arrived home his wife was still wearing the dress she had worn for Christmas.

Now Bert's father-in-law, Captain Fred Harris had left Conyer the day after Bert with a load of bricks for London. Fred had not got far when he sighted a loaded barge coming towards him. 'That looks like the *Rutland*.' said Fred Harris to his mate. 'Can't be,' said his mate, 'hasn't had time.' 'I know it is.' said Fred, 'Bet you ten bob.' Sure enough, it was Bert Webb pushing the *Rutland* along, so making his father-in-law richer by ten bob (50p).

Bert told me that Richardson's Dock at Conyer was a bad place for a loaded barge. The mud had so much suction that a loaded craft had difficulty in floating when the tide came in, so much so that the water would be well over the decks before a barge lifted. This was common at other places on the coast. To break the suction they would pass a chain under the barges and work it to and fro allowing the water to work under the barges bottom thereby breaking the suction.

Bert could remember Richardson's crane unloading flints in the dock for road making. He also told me that his father-in-law had taken Conyer cement to London to be used for building the Victoria and Albert Memorial.

Bert told me of the time when Captain 'Bones' Wylie went into the Ship Inn and asked the landlord Bill Foster to give him a stiff whisky. The landlord had never seen him in such a state and asked him if anything was wrong. 'He'll be the death of me.' was the reply. The 'he' in this instance was Bert's brother Norman, who was sailing with 'Bones' as mate. It appears that it had been a bitterly cold morning with a heavy frost. 'Bones' and Norman had rowed the barge's boat out to the barge which was anchored in South Deep. Both of them climbed aboard, each thinking the other had made the boat fast to the barge. It was not until they saw it floating away that they realised what had happened. 'Bones' then got into a rage as they had no means of recovering the boat. Norman told him not to worry; took off his clothes and dived overboard, swam to the boat and brought it back. 'Bones' thought the bitterly cold water would kill Norman, and he suffered the shock more than Norman did.

Bert Webb and Ted Beacon, both retired, are now the only two sailing barge captains from Conyer still living in the area; strange for a village where once upon a time most families had a father or son at sea, and yes, even wives.

Chapter 4

The Oyster Fisheries of Max Holman

At one time oysters used to be cultivated in the Swale off the mouth of Conyer Creek. Here was the oyster merchanting business of Max Holman which employed a fair percentage of Conyer people. His great niece told me that his name was originally Ullman, but was changed at the beginning of WWI because of its Teutonic origins. Amongst those employed were Alec Banks, who was the foreman, Ben 'Punt' Ennew, the donkey cart driver, Charlie Wyatt, Tom Arnold, a Mr. Neeston, and the Captain of the steamboat, Mr. Andrews.

I spent an evening with Peter Parrish who had celebrated his eighty-fifth birthday the previous week. I had been told that Ben 'Punt' Ennew had lodged with his family, which turned out to be true. That house had been in the Parrish family for seventy four years; they had moved in when Alec Banks moved out. Peter's memory was still very sharp and some of his tales had tears running from my eyes; it was some time before I could take down notes.

Ben had been in charge of the donkey cart which used to take the odd lots of oysters to the station; the bulk was bought by Harry French, the local carter and pub landlord. The donkey had been sent by rail to Teynham, and was a good looking animal, being a dark coated variety, strong and a fast goer. Max Holman had also sent down a fine set of harness embellished with all the brass trimmings which, I was told looked very smart on the donkey. The cart was a small affair of light construction with a flat body, and the donkey and cart were kept at the rear of the Parrish home. The stable is still there to this day.

It appears that some days there was no work for the donkey and cart so the animal would be left in the stable. It also appears that a trio of hard working brickies decided that the donkey needed some exercise on its days off. After coming off shift work they would call at Mr. Parrish's home and ask if they could borrow the donkey and cart; it being all right, they would harness up and all three would mount the cart. One of them, Alf Smith by name, was a tall man who had long legs. He would have to sit on the back of the cart with legs dangling, almost touching the ground; the other two would sit either side and they would then go on a tour of the local pubs. Most men in those days were hard workers and, it seems, also hard drinkers; perhaps the only means they had of unwinding. One could always find which pub this trio was at by seeing the donkey outside chewing away at a loaf of bread which they had either cadged or bought off the landlord.

The Oyster Company had its oyster beds in the Swale each side of Fowley Island, where they bred at least three different varieties. Between the mainland and Fowley Island they bred an oyster called Ports (Portuguese or non-native oysters) which were

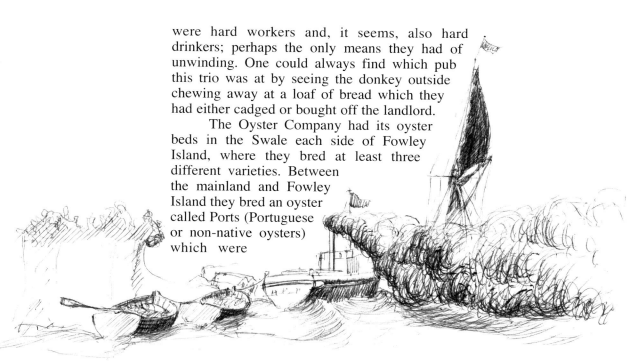

Oyster boats being towed out of the Creek.

large ones. Mr. Parrish told me that they used to fry these and they made a delicious meal. Between Fowley and Sheppey they bred Natives, a better class of oyster. Ben 'Punt' Ennew preferred his oysters baked in the oven.

At the foot of the sea wall, below high water mark, the mud was covered with oyster nurseries on trays. Mr. Parrish used to watch them spread something in the trays like dust, which I assume must have been the spat. It is difficult to determine the extent of Max Holman's fishery: In Jacobs' The History of Faversham it states that the Faversham Oyster Company's grounds start at the place called Teynham Robbs upon the south, and by west to a place called Black Shore, along Teynham Gutt eastwards and from Teynham Gutt along by Ride Ferry Way down to a place called Stinkes Nasse.

We know where Teynham Gutt is, but the other places have to be guessed at. The breeding pits were on Fowley Island and can still be seen. The Company had a large building close to where the Target stood; it had three rooms for the workmen, who were mainly Essex men; one room was lavishly furnished and was set aside for Max Holman, where he spent many weekends. Later the workmen moved into the village. The boats used by the oystermen were called skiffs which were about twenty feet long. There was also a steam boat which dredged when it had nothing else to do. Its main purpose was to spread new batches of oysters over the beds.

A large number of oysters were brought from Essex by barge which were added to the beds to improve the strain when breeding. These barges were unloaded by brickies who were glad of the extra money.

After being dredged and sorted the oysters would then be loaded into the boats and rowed up the creek, or towed by the steamboat to the packing shed which stood at the Warren. Here they were packed into sacks of so many dozens weighing about twenty pounds. The packing shed at the Warren was the last link with the oyster trade.

When I worked at the shipyard we used it as a store for boats gear, sails and spars. It had two rooms: one, which had a brick fireplace, we used as a mess room at one time and it was very cosy with a fire going on cold days. Unfortunately someone broke into it one night and set light to it at a time when it was full of boat gear belonging to a Dutch barge called *Sirius* which belonged to a Mr. Constantine (See page 47). Nothing could be saved and afterwards only the fireplace stood. Another link with the past had gone forever.

The Captain of the oyster company's steam boat was a Mr. Andrews who lived in Conyer. Sometimes he could be seen giving a tow to the mud barge *Liza*, whose master, Captain Radley, also lived in Conyer.

This is an account of how oysters were sorted given to the late Mr. March by a Whitstable fisherman. From Edgar J. March's book Inshore Craft of Britain in the Days of Sail and Oar I quote: 'Pearly counters the size of a shilling infest oysters less than a year old, some covered with red pimples, Quats, two years old the size of half crowns, only four year olds picked out and thrown into baskets, will live about ten years, best at five, age told by layers outside bottom shell, perfect yellow circle at small end of fan is one year, then three successive brown pearly semicircles represents three other years, and rough fringe round outer edge is one more year old, four years for general eating.' The account, of course, is written as it was told in the East Kent dialect, now so infrequently heard.

Once again I refer to Charles Igglesdon. Talking to old bargemen at Conyer he was told that you could purchase them, rather small perhaps but of excellent flavour at the rate of sixpence a quarter of a hundred, 'and you would know' said his informant, with a smile, 'a quarter of a hundred meant thirty in those days.' Oysters at less than a farthing each!

A man elderly then who was engaged in trimming up a barge told me that 'brood oysters are difficult to obtain nowadays.' and yet he himself was one of a crew that used to go to Falmouth and Jersey and flush up 'brood' from outside rocks; they were then brought up the Swale and cultivated. With a twinkle in his eye he said that 'Although they can no longer be found in the Swale, sometimes a few of them swim out from Whitstable beds and lose themselves near 'ere and you can't send them back!'

The Oyster Company also owned a Bawley boat called the *Bessie* which the local men used to borrow to go trawling between South Deep and the mouth of Faversham Creek. It used to be a good place to trawl soles.

The Bawley.

Chapter 5

The Barge Trades

Shipping had traded to Conyer for a very long time. In the 18th. and early 19th. centuries the trading vessels would have been brigs, hoys, cutters and a selection of smaller craft rigged in the fashion of chalk and lime barges of that period. Most of the vessels using the creek would have been owned at other ports. Certainly there is no mention of any barges or lighters being around at Conyer in 1795, when James Tappenden compiled his return for the port of Faversham, including in it all barges and lighters owned on Faversham and Milton creeks.

Bagshaw's Directory of 1847 mentions that vessels of 150 tons burthen came up to Conyer Creek. Such vessels would have been registered at around 70 tons. By way of comparison Chamber's barge *Murton* of 1866 was 39 tons registered 80 tons burthen, so the vessels using Conyer Creek could have been coasting hoys, collier brigs or schooners.

The Directory does not mention anyone in Conyer or Teynham actually connected with shipping trades, but then such directories were not noted for their accuracy. What it probably means is that such shipping as used the creek also used the services of a local agent, probably from Sittingbourne. The Directory mentions the following persons who were in business at either Conyer Quay or Tenham (as it was then written) excluding Lewson Street or Greenstreet.

Sar. Beacon. Victualler of The Ship Inn, Conyer.
John Bourne. Farmer, Frognal.
Rev. Wm. Datkins, Curate.
Stephen Hunt, Carpenter.
Joseph Kent, Farmer.
Wm. Roper, Farmer.
Henry Silver, Blacksmith.

At the Plough Inn, Greenstreet, was Frederick Honeyball, victualler, who probably acted as agent and ship victualler for vessels using the Creek. The brigs and schooners of that time used to take on ballast at Conyer for their return trips. This was gravel dug out of a local field. The larger vessels needed great amounts of ballast put into their holds after they had unloaded their cargoes, which was necessary to give them stability to sail when light laden. The ballast was then taken out before they loaded their next cargo.

The barges, of course, were flat bottomed and needed no ballast. Coal was required for hearths and for various mechanical devices in use in the surrounding countryside, including the steam engine which powered the Sidders Brothers' flourmill.

The Blaxland family were farmers, shipowners, and merchants with various members of the family ensconced at many ports in Kent.

By far the largest of Alfred Marconi White's Conyer built craft was the 97 ton ketch barge *Olympia*. Built in 1902 she was to have but a short life, being run down off Deal, Kent, by a steamer when laden with 220 tons of pitch for Boulogne on 13th. March 1918. After WWII she was found by divers to be remarkably intact, and complete with her cargo. Her brass wheel boss, inscribed 'White of Teynham' was removed and brought ashore. Before her demise she was sold to Samuel West of Gravesend, for whom White had built the *Ronald West* in 1903, at 73 tons the second largest of White's output. The *Ronald West* was sunk in Harwich harbour after a collision with the S.S. *Crossbill* in November 1936, being raised and then broken up in 1938 at Pin Mill.

At Whitstable they were big shipowners. In the 1860s John Blaxland was farming at Teynham and Edward Blaxland had established himself as a coal merchant. No doubt, many of the colliers visiting the creek were some of the smaller colliers owned by Blaxlands at Whitstable.

Other local coal merchants were Honeyballs, who later had the big ketch barge *Olympia* built at Conyer, and Walter Kimmins, who was also agent to the Kent Coal Company. Both had depots at Teynham Station and undoubtedly had cargoes brought in. Fred Honeyball of Teynham was at that time manager of his company's coal wharf at Crown Quay, Sittingbourne, and also looked after the Conyer/Teynham side. Kimmins is a name I will mention later, when in 1862 a Mr. James Kimmins leased the Conyer corn mill. Frequently, merchants of this period were corn and coal merchants combined.

But long before the coal trade was established 'Conyers Quay' was 'much used for the shipping of corn and goods from this part of the country, near which there is an oil mill established, lately belonging to the Bests'. So wrote the historian Ireland in the 18th. century. These cargoes would have been oil from Bests' mill, flour from Sidders Brothers smock mill, and corn and agricultural produce from surrounding farms.

In the early 19th. century local farms and landowners included the Chambers, John Bourne, John Kent, and William Roper at lower Teynham. A Sir S. Chambers had his seat at Woodstock near Sittingbourne, and the family were later barge owners at Conyer and Faversham. Later farmers were the Mercer's of Rodmersham who took over a wharf on Conyer Creek. With the orchards surrounding Teynham there was also an export of hard fruits, especially apples and pears, and also cherries for London. These farmers would also have had a requirement for straw muck-outs to be used as dressing for their lands. Another cargo which was brought into the creek was oyster brood for relaying. In the late 18th. century smacks sailed regularly to Holland with exports of Faversham Native Oysters.

I think that the large smock mill at Conyer Quay must have been located on the bank where Quay Cottages now stand, or possibly on the site behind the cottages. This mill was worked by two brothers with the name of Sidders who were obviously very busy, always with plenty of corn to grind. It was a source of wonder to many people how it was that the sails of the mill kept going round even when there was no wind. The brothers Sidders were enterprising men and had an early steam engine fitted and connected it up to the sails, so when there was no wind they would start the steam engine up and the sails would then act as a fly wheel. But then steam came to be fitted into many mills in East Kent early in the 19th. century.

Unfortunately the Sidders Brothers were ruined owing to a heavy fall in the price of wheat at the close of the Crimean War. There was another mill near Conyer owned by Mr. H. Divers but not much seems to be known of this miller, or where his mill stood.

It seems remarkable that none of the older people of Conyer knew much about these mills, or if they did they never talk about them.

Their parents must have remembered them; the Crimean War ended in 1856 and it is unlikely that they were pulled down straight away. Mrs. Selby states in her book that Mr. William Roper delivered wheat into this mill at £6 a quarter early last century; this seems a fantastic price for wheat all those years ago!

In searching the archives at County Hall, Maidstone, I read through three sets of deeds relating to a corn mill at Conyer. One was dated 1826; 'Edward Amos and others under the will of Hope Amos agree to lease the mill to Mr. James Kimmins for £60 per annum for 14 years.'

One interesting item in the agreement was that Mr. Kimmins was to tar the weather board section of the mill every two years, using only the best quality tar (no wonder these old wooden buildings used to stand for year after year). This lease had a memo added, 'that by Indenture dated 22nd. May 1828 this lease is assigned for the remainder of the term unto Thomas Weller, miller of Hollingbourne.'

I then found the lease mentioned in the memo, it was headed 'Indentures between James Kimmins of Teynham and Edwards Amos of Norton, that the mill in Conyer be leased at £60 per annum to Thomas Weller of Hollingbourne, Miller.' The reading was almost word for word as the previous one.

The third one was dated 28th. December, 1839, between Richard Amos of Oare and John Robert Divers of Oare, to lease to William Henry Divers, miller of Teynham, the mill at £60 per annum. To commence 6th. January, 1840, for 14 years until its expiration in 1854.

Another earlier deed to the mill was dated 1762 to 1829. There was also an oil mill at Conyer. This oil mill was owned by Maudisley Best who had land at Barrow Green and Castle Wood, Teynham, and also much land in Lynsted around 1740. He also owned a brewery believed to be the one which was later known as George Beer and Rigden, who's beer was known as 'Kent's Best'. Was this in honour of Maudisley Best I wonder?

From the early part of the 19th. century bricks became the principle cargo to be carried out of Conyer Creek, and this trade was carried on until not so many years ago. Second to the brick trade came cement. Roman cement was invented in the late 18th. century and was certainly produced on Milton Creek and at Faversham shortly afterwards. Portland cement, although patented in the 1820s was not in production until the next decade. Roman cement was made from boulders dredged off Sheppey, and it was reasonable to assume that this product was being manufactured at Conyer at least by 1850.

The Postal and Commercial Directory for 1867 records that 'Extensive Roman and Portland Cement work and brick making is extensively carried on.' and it is recorded that the manufacture of bricks and cement had been continued for quite some years.

The principal manufacturers in that year were:
1. Braney, Withes and Lucas, Brickmakers. Manager Mr. Howard.
2. Harland & Brewer, Brickers (also at Chislehurst).

3. Charles Richardson, Portland & Roman Cement Manufacturer & Brickmaker of Conyer Quay; Brunswick Wharf, Vauxhall and also of 6 South Wharf, Paddington.

4. Millichamp and Chambers, Brickmakers at Frognal Brickworks.

The industry must have been extensive, as one Mr. D. Bolton, employed himself an engineer. In those days there was a village shop, kept by William Graham.

In the Archives at Maidstone are the title deeds of the Teynham Brick Company. The company paid £500 to Alfred Stacey for a piece of land called Osiers Barn Field, which ran from the railway to Osiers Road. It was eleven acres, nine perches. The piece of land had been leased to Mr. Stacey by James Lake. It also states that the Teynham Brick Company were to pay Mr. Stacey one shilling and sixpence per thousand royalty. Written into the deed was that the company was to be allowed to lease part of the wharf at Conyer belonging to James Lake. A small hand-drawn map was added to the side of the deeds showing a portion of wharf and water but it gave no indication as to where the wharf was situated. The wharf and surrounding land was owned by James Lake, but an interesting thing about this map was the fact that some land overlapping the wharf was owned by Sidders. This could be the same Sidders who had the windmill in Conyer Quay. These deeds were dated 1866 and this is about the time the Sidders brothers stopped using the mill, but the indications are that the brothers were working the brickfields here at least up until that date.

The East Kent Gazette for 1866 records that a barge, the *Industry* had sunk in unfortunate circumstances with bricks from Teynham, bound for London, when she was struck by a steamer off Coalhouse Point and went down with her cargo. The mate was drowned.

The Chambers family interests ranged from agriculture to bricks. The Frognal brickworks was served by the firm's sailing barges. At one time there were two barges named *Frognal*. In 1866 Mr. H. Chambers of Millichamp & Chambers had the barge *Murton* built for him by William Mantle and Son of Crown Quay, the Sittingbourne barge builders.

Who or what Murton was, I do not know, but there was a local family of that name, one of whom had once been a bookseller in Milton Regis, and there were others who farmed at Faversham and Eastling. Later the Murtons were coal merchants and commissioners at Faversham. The barge was launched on Wednesday 18th. April, of 39 tons and measured 72 feet by 14 feet by $5^{1}/_{2}$ feet. At her launching she was described as reflecting 'considerable credit on her builders.' The dimensions of the *Murton* make her a long, low and narrow hull, and many barges were built to this size to enable them to navigate the Regents Canal. Her master was James Wybrow who 21 years later met his end in an unfortunate way, falling off the top of a tramcar in Deptford. She was topsail rigged and was one of 18 barges to compete in the Topsail Class of The 1867 Sailing Barge Match. I do not know she fared in the race.

The bricks and cement made at Conyer were used for building houses and other properties in London. Most manufacturers had their own depots in London at which the barges unloaded. These were on the Thames, its tributaries - the Wey and the Lea, and canals like the Regents and the Grand Surrey, giving fairly comprehensive distribution.

Charles Richardson had a depot on the Regents Canal, at South Wharf Paddington, during the time that North London was expanding, and many of his barges worked into the canal system. Later some of Eastwoods' barges ran regularly through the Regents Canal, squeezing into the locks and 'legging' their way through the long tunnels such as Maida Vale.

From the mid part of the 19th. century until the Great War much of the barge traffic to Conyer was in the hands of the Richardson family, whose fortunes became so closely twinned with Eastwoods that it is not always possible to separate them.

In the 1860s Charles Richardson founded two businesses. The Conyer Cement Works, which was sited on the quay, and the Teynham Field Brickworks which was near the railway station. Charles Richardson was also in business at Vauxhall, the receiving end of the freightline, where his barges unloaded their cargoes. He utilised the dock at Conyer, and later the Teynham brickworks was connected to the creek by means of a narrow gauge railway.

In about 1855 Charles, Rowley, and Walter Richardson combined their interests with various other firms of brick and cement manufacturers - to form an association with Eastwoods. Charles Richardson then dropped out of the picture, some of his barges passed to Eastwoods direct, others to Rowley or to Walter Thomas of Vauxhall. The latter continued to manage his own craft, but Rowley's with those of Eastwoods own came to be managed by Eastwoods manager Arthur Francis Bryne.

Charles Richardson's first barges seem to have been the stumpy *Sophia* of 1856, and the round bowed *Frederick & Mary Ann* of 1852, both probably acquired second hand in the early 1860s. For his first orders he went to a Mr. Edwin Burgess of Queenborough to have built the *Eliza*, launched by Miss Beaton of Conyer on 26th. June 1866, and the *Charles* which was launched later that year.

Here Burgess ran into trouble. He had started in a grand style in 1865 as a ship, barge and boat builder, mast, block and pump maker, at the yard formerly occupied by Japter, James and Page. He inserted fine advertisements to solicit business in the East Kent Gazette, and naturally that newspaper went along to record the launching of the *Eliza*, which was quite an affair as the yard was away from the quay and the barge had to be launched across the roadway. Alas Burgess had underestimated the cost of building and he had to file a petition for bankruptcy even when *Charles* was still on the ways.

Charles Richardson then acquired the Murston built *Frank* of 1870, the *Ruby* of 1873, the *William & Eleanor*, *Swift* of 1874, *Swallow* of 1877, *Osprey* of 1881, and *Plover* 1884, most of these barges passing in the 1880s direct to Eastwoods.

The 'stumpie' rigged *Charles*, once tiller steered like the barge to the right, is seen in the dock c.1890. The high tide has submerged the tramway to the west of the dock.

W.T. Richardson, of Brunswick Wharf, Vauxhall, generally kept his barges out of Eastwoods amalgamation. He had the *William* built for him at Sittingbourne in 1872, and then three barges from Bird at Conyer, *Jeffie* and *Lydia* in 1874 and *Phoebe* in 1876, and then took over two of Charles Richardson's barges the *Eliza* and the *Charles*.

Rowley Richardson's barges were the old *George & Ellen* of 1845 which he acquired from Woods, along with the Faversham built *Arthur & Eliza* built at Faversham in 1862, the *Frank* of 1870, (from Charles Richardson), another older barge the round-bowed *Frederick & Mary Ann* of 1852, the *Active* of 1864, the *Mabel* which he had built at Conyer in 1873, which R.W. Richardson seemed to have had a share in, and finally the *Heron* of 1884.

While Eastwoods expanded their business at Conyer's Butterfly and Klondyke Works, W.T. and Rowley continued to own their own barges, some later passed on to Eastwoods, but four of W.T.'s craft *Jeffie, Lydia, Phoebe* and *Eliza* carried on for Alexander Richardson, also of Brunswick Wharf, Vauxhall. I presume there was a connection between Brunswick Wharf and our own Brunswick Field and The Brunswick Arms.

Eastwood had new barges built at Conyer, Faversham, Halstow, and Otterham which carried on serving the creek into the 1930s.

In 1919 Richardsons sold the 'Top Field' brickworks and the Conyer dock to Eastwoods, all that remains of Richardson interests at Conyer are the dock and the now derelict cement works - oh yes and

Three kilns of the Cement Works, seen here around 1935 beyond the barge yacht *Waveney*, were demolished by Aylward Bros. during the Second World War to provide brick rubble for runways at airfields.

two old carved tiller bars, which Colonel Blackden found recently when he had the old stables at the head of the dock demolished. The scroll work and carving are intact, although they require restoration, the carved panels in the fashion of the 1860s and 1870s bear the names *Charles* and *William*.

At the head of Richardson's Dock were the cement mills whose washbacks ran parallel with the road. At the back of the washbacks stood six kilns where the cement was fired.

First a layer of faggots was laid, covered with a layer of coal, followed by a layer of mud mixture from the washbacks. This sequence was repeated until the kiln was full to the top. The holes in the kiln were then bricked up and the lot set fire to. After being burnt the kiln was left to cool, then the holes were unbricked and the burnt mud taken to the mill to be ground into powder. At the front of the single story building there were double doors opening out onto the road. The bagged cement was wheeled through these to be slid down

The cement mill doors from where cement was barrowed across the road to the dock, then tipped down a chute into the hold of the barge. The Cement Mill closed down about 1914 after 60 years of production. This 1970s photograph of the mill also shows the new housing which overlooks the dock.

a chute into barges. These doors are still there now and a few years ago once could still see the chute at the edges of the wharf.

Loading must have been a filthy job: the cement was in jute sacks of two hundredweight, and after sliding down the chute and hitting the bottom there was a permanent fog of dust. The last three kilns were demolished by Aylward Brothers in about 1940, and the rubble was used at local airfields. Demolition proved to be a tough job as all the bricks had welded together with the continual firing. In the engine house at the back of the mill was a large steam engine, which had supplied all the power to the mill; this was broken up in the summer of 1939 and taken to Dover as scrap. Its destination was Germany. I often wonder how much of it Adolph Hitler sent us back!

This steam engine had been driven for many years by Mr. Ernest Harvey, a very clever engineer and millwright. I spent many hours with him in is workshop. He was the first man to have a motor powered boat in Conyer, which with many others lay at the parish wharf.

Richardson's locomotive was of a type built by Aveling in 1888, maker's number 1708. It had a 2-2-0 wheel arrangement and a wheel diameter of 5 feet. It had but one cylinder 8 inches diameter by 12 inches and ran on 3 foot 9 inch gauge track.

About halfway along Richardson's Dock there was a wash mill which pumped the mud across the road by means of an overhead chute into the washbacks. The mud barges unloaded close to this wash mill.

Mr. Parrish told me the tale of how Mr. Frost's donkey changed its colour at the mill. It appears that Mr. Frost, who was landlord of the Ship Inn, had a very dark, good-looking donkey which pulled a very smart looking donkey cart. The cart had a woven wickerwork body, all very attractive, and when coupled with the donkey made a very colourful turnout. One day it stood outside the Inn all ready to take the Landlord out as soon as he had got rid of his customers. But they had other ideas about this and they set about getting him drunk, a task in which they succeeded. In the meantime, some of them had taken the donkey out of the cart and led him to the wash mill where they gave him a coat of liquid mud; they then took him back and harnessed him up to the cart again. By the time the Landlord was ready to go, the donkey had dried a dirty white colour. They then sat the Landlord in the cart and watched him try to drive away. Being the worse for drink was bad enough, but the fact that this was another instance when the motive power, this time a donkey, had been turned around in a cart's shafts, made it all the more difficult for the Landlord to get started!

At one time there were four brickfields in Conyer each loading their bricks at various wharves on the creek. The Conyer Field loaded their bricks at the Butterfly Wharf. The brickfield used to be nearer to the wharf than it is now, and the present works is the third to occupy this locality. This was a busy wharf. One could always see craft loading or unloading, and many times I have been sent to the wharf to do minor repairs to the barges. On very cold days I would climb up in the cab of the steam crane to warm my hands. At that time Fred Hodges was the crane driver, with Bill Jones.

Loading at Conyer was nearly all bricks. Unloading would be 'Roughstuff' or, as we know it, the contents of the London ash bins. Also delivered was moulding sand, coal, and mud, dug out of Fowley Island or the surrounding mud holes, by men using a 'fly' tool. The 'muddies' would stand on the mud, one each side of the barge, and with a very quick wrist action would fill the barge with long narrow slabs of mud.

Eastwoods' *Durham* was built at Conyer by Alfred Marconi White in 1899. Here she has been relegated to the mud work. She carries a rudimentary sailplan, and never had to stray beyond the muddy creeks and rills of the Swale shoreline when this picture was taken in 1954.

The 'Top Field', as the Teynham field was known, loaded its bricks at the dock opposite the old cement works. The bricks here were loaded on flat trucks pulled two at a time by horses down the tramway to Conyer. The tramway was on a slightly falling gradient which made it easier work for the horses. Before this the trucks of bricks had been worked by a steam locomotive which had a tall chimney, in the fashion of the steam traction engines which ran on the road. The steam locomotive was driven by Mr. Jack Taylor. When the working was taken over by horses Jack was offered a job driving locomotives on the Southern Railway but declined and went to work in the brickfields.

At the Butterfly Wharf the whole truck load of bricks used to be lowered straight into the barge's hold and then unloaded and stacked by hand. But loading at the dock had to be handled from the trucks standing on the wharf. Here the first man in the gang would pick up five bricks off the truck, throw them to a second man standing on the deck of the barge, who threw them to a third man standing in the hold of the barge, who then stacked them tightly in the hold. There were often two men in the barge, so that as the distance got greater they could pass the bricks to one another. 'Roughstuff' and sand was unloaded from the barges by hand, then pulled to Top Field by horses.

Two brickfields at Frognal also brought their bricks to Conyer. They had a tramway which came in at the head of the creek onto Mercer's Wharf where bricks were loaded, and coal, 'roughstuff' and sand were unloaded.

Horse dung and straw muck-outs from the numerous stables in London were shipped by barge and unloaded onto the public wharf in front of the Ship Inn. Apparently every one within two miles knew when the load came in. 'Darkie' Mills told me that when a dung barge was up, you had to keep your hand over your beer in the Ship Inn otherwise as fast as you drank, your beer topped itself up with flies. It was a local joke that the flies were so thick that if you happened to get drunk it was impossible to fall over. Potter Oyler were the last people to unload dung at Parish Wharf. They had markets in London, which meant they had horses and stables, so it was policy to use their own dung which had to be brought out of London.

Between Conyer village and the Butterfly Wharf there was a small dock called Blacketts (see picture page 19). Here hay, straw and other crops for market along the coast, were loaded and dung was unloaded. You can still see the outline of this dock, but it is almost silted up level with the surrounding mud.

Talking to a former barge captain who has come to live at Conyer in his retirement, he told me that many years ago he delivered ballast to Conyer for the tramway; this must have been when the steam locomotive worked it, as when it was worked by horses, if my memory serves me right, it was ballasted by brickdust. He also tells me that he had delivered dung to the wharf when other freights were short.

One of the last barges to deliver dung to Conyer was the *Ernest & Ada*. She was what was termed a 'tore out', fit for nothing else except perhaps 'roughstuff'. She was by then a real 'old timer', having been built by Kemp at Paglesham in Essex as early as 1865.

The old Conyer Field occupies a substantial acreage at the mouth of the creek. The frontage to The Swale can just be seen in the top left of this photograph taken in 1968, though the Butterfly Wharf which served the works is out of shot. By the time of this picture manufacture had already ceased, but the Redland Works, between Eastwoods' Conyer Field and the village, was still in production and stocks of bricks can be seen beyond the buildings.

Chapter 6

Brickmaking at the Conyer Field

As a schoolboy I had to pass one of Eastwoods' earth holes on my way to school. Here men dug out the earth by hand and loaded it into horse drawn carts. This was one of their smaller earth holes and not being far from the brickfield did not warrant a tramway. Most earth holes had tramways laid up to the heading on which side tipping trucks were pushed up close to the workings where they were filled by the men with large shovels. The same method was used in the chalk pits except that the bulk of the chalk was loaded with a stone fork, and crumb that was left was shovelled up.

Usually the earth and the chalk was then drawn by a locomotive to the washmill where it was mixed into a slurry and pumped into washbacks; large areas of land embanked with earth and bricks walls, sometimes as far as two miles or more away from the brickfield. The slurry was pumped through a six inch cast iron pipeline, and with a system of wooden chutes it was evenly distributed in the washbacks so that the solids did not all settle in one place.

Digging the chalk around 1928 for brick making. Like most tasks in the brick and cement trades, clothing soon took on the colour of the raw materials being worked. This was mixed with earth at the washmill.

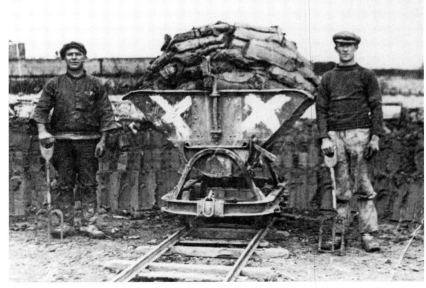

These large slices of clay needed tough men to dig and load them into skips year after year in all weathers. The man on the right, Mr. Julius Kemsley started work at Conyer in 1907 and dug clay for 54 years. He claims to have dug more clay than any man living. Julius is still alive and well over 80 and has many yarns to tell of the old days.

The wash was then left to settle for about nine months. The water evaporated leaving a sticky cheese-like clay which was dug out with a three pronged fork having a sharp blade across the bottom of the prongs. I have watched men using these forks, called 'cuckles'. They had a rhythmical movement of the arms and body slicing out large chunks of clay up to 18 inches long and depositing them into the truck all in one movement. The chunks of clay must have weighed 50 pounds or more and by the time the truck was loaded it was as high as their heads.

Some of these men like Julius Kemsley spent most of their working lives digging clay. It developed them into strong men early which enabled them to carry on until they retired. Julius who is in his eighties is still upright and gets about well for a man who claims he has dug more clay than any man living.

After the clay had been loaded into the side tipping trucks it was pushed out of the washback onto the tramway and hooked onto a continuously moving wire cable which pulled it to the factory up an incline to be tipped into a mill which chewed it up and mixed it ready for the moulder to mould his bricks. After being moulded the bricks were stacked on trays on special trucks which went through the driers at a slow rate, being dried by hot air to get as much moisture as possible out before being burnt.

After coming out of the drier the bricks were taken off the drier trucks and stacked on larger trucks, a mould being used to make sure that they could pass through the tunnel kiln where they were burnt. This was a continuous system as a freshly loaded truck was pushed in it automatically pushed a truck of burnt bricks out at the other end. Sometimes the bricks were red hot which made sorting difficult. After sorting they were either stacked for stock, loaded onto lorries, or taken to Butterfly Wharf to be loaded into barges.

A skip of clay about to be hooked onto the wire hauling cable. The track system was extensive; in this picture the double track is met at 90° by a single track from the right, and a small turntable under the skip wagon allowed it to be rotated and aligned with the 'main line'.

Green (unfired) bricks are loaded, with gaps in between each brick to allow air circulation, onto trolleys which passed slowly through the driers.

A three man 'crowding' gang building up a truck of dried bricks prior to it going through the cowl to be burnt. All the pictures on this page were taken around 1928.

The Butterfly Wharf was the wharf for the Conyer Field. Barges were loaded at 'piece-work rates' at the wharf. All stowing was by hand which meant the men had to work very hard at the best of time; a soul destroying job for a pair of loaders, one of whom told me of this hardship shared with his mate. It appears that they were loading a barge with bricks that were very hot straight from sorting. The barge had been fully loaded with 40,000 bricks when smoke was seen to be coming from the hold. The manager was sent for and after inspecting the cargo and finding it to be very hot, he turned to the loaders and said 'You b..... fools should have known better, you can unload them and reload them for nothing.' After unloading the bricks the keelson of the barge was found to be alight.

The same man told me that on passing the office one day the manager came out and stopped them. 'Did you see the barge that came in on the tide?' The two men said that they had. 'I want it loaded by the tide tomorrow afternoon at 4.30 p.m.' The load was for 44,000

Some chalk arrived by barge. At Richardson's Dock a cargo is unloading, those aboard the barge filling the steam crane's bucket, except the barge's skipper who watches, leaning on a pile of hatch covers aft of the main hold. The photograph dates from around 1912.

bricks which were urgently wanted in London. The two of them started the next morning. The skipper of the barge had gone home but the mate was still aboard. The mate told them that his skipper was expecting two days at home and that he would be b..... mad if they got her loaded that day. Working like b..... slaves they got her loaded. They then helped the mate put the hatches on. By this time the skipper who had been recalled, arrived. He called them all the names he could remember for losing him a day's rest. On passing the office on their way home that night the manager came out and gave them a pound each. It is hard to imagine why men had to work so hard in those not so far off days.

The ability of (some) sailormen to swear reminds me of what Sir Walter Runciman wrote of them in his book Collier Brigs and their Sailors. 'Coals were brought to London from Newcastle in sailing vessels which were too old for deep sea charter. These were crewed by Geordie or North Country sailors mostly; tough hard swearing men made so by the very nature of their work which was dirty, hard and

Loading coals for the brickfield boilers. The tramway wagons fulfil yet another role. The spars of sailing barges are a frequent back-drop to pictures of Conyer and its industries.

Cutting hard bricks from burrs. Burrs were a number of bricks welded together by heat in the brick burning process, essentially waste, but much in demand for building walls.

Charlie Smeed, engine driver at the Conyer Brickfield. All the pictures on this page were taken around 1928.

very risky as most of it was carried out in the winter months, many colliers were wrecked on the east coast each year.'

Sir Walter writes that the collier sailors always thought that they were superior to the Thames bargemen, and when sailing in the Thames would swear at and insult the bargemen. Sir Walter goes on to say 'Then the flowers of bargee speech were sent flying with passionate force at the Geordies, who were gifted with insufficient language adequately to meet the attack. They were called names that the bargee specialised in, which never have been and never can be printed. The attack was not only on themselves but on their parents and on the character of their ancestors, covering distant ages. The North country men had no vocabulary that could match it.'

In spite of what Sir Walter Runciman said (who was a Geordie sailor most of his life), I have sailed with bargemen that have been God fearing and quiet of manner, and most of those that I have had the pleasure to sail with recently have been just so.

The remains of Conyer Brickfields shaft which was dropped in 1969. Built by W. Austin and Sonny Austin, it was 185 ft. high. Ethel Whitehead was the first woman to go to the top of it. Mrs. Spratt told me that when she went to the top she was surprised at the wonderful view that met her eyes when she peered over the top. The ladders were on the inside, being the ones used by builders.

Chapter 7

Steam Chests and Trunnel Mutes

I often think of the prospects of the youth about to start working for his living in this automated age. What an uninteresting choice of jobs confront him. At least when I started there were jobs with plenty of interest, even though they were getting scarce, and I chose the job that interested me, barge building. Although a dying trade at least it was probably one of the most interesting of the rural crafts still existing.

When I joined the Conyer barge yard in 1935, it was then managed by Arthur White, and the building of sailing barges had ceased. *Annie Byford* had been the last one and that was back in 1916. Although we were then building non-sailing craft we were always surrounded by sailing barges, as they continued to come up to the yard for repair, refitting, or to be doubled and we carried out this work in addition to our new building.

Among the barges which came to us for repair I recall the *Annie Byford, John Byford, Castanet, Bankside, Venta, George, Mermaid, Waveney, Glasgow, Sunbeam, Shannon*, and the Eastwoods' barges that traded to Conyer.

On some of them quite detailed works had to be carried out; typical examples were the *Castanet* and *Bankside* which belonged to Colonel R.C. Bingham, both of which became war casualties. The former was the first to come to us, for a complete refit to conform to Board of Trade Coasting Standards. The *Bankside* followed; we had to put two new chine keelsons in her and a new steel main keelson. Removing the original wooden keelson was hard work. It was cut in six foot lengths, by a cross-cut saw, one man on each end but the chine keelsons had to be cut out by a hand saw with only about six inches of movement. As the barge was on the blocks at the time the long bolts were backed out. It was a very tedious job. We then fitted the new chine keelsons as per the originals. It seemed a never ending job driving the bolts upwards, and when they were first entered there was only about 4 inches of clearance between the hard bottom of the berth and the head of the bolt. The maul was turned on its side and the bolt was tapped until clearance allowed it to be used in the normal way. You either had to sit on a board, or kneel, depending on how the aches attacked you.

Venta, originally named *Jachin* was a powerful coaster from John Howard's yard at Maldon, Essex. Here she is seen retired from cargo carrying and converted to a yacht, taking part in the 1951 Medway Barge Sailing Match.

Colonel Bingham permitted his Captains to stay on board all the time that work was in progress, so that if anything did not suit them it could be altered there and then. Colonel Bingham also had another barge, the *George*, which was converted into a yacht barge. Eli Head was Captain of her, complete with blue jersey with the name *George* emblazoned across his chest in red lettering.

The repair work was always complicated. With *Bankside* we had to refasten her, fit a number of new planks, one new leeboard, replace part of the decking, fit a new head ledge and a new section of rail and supply a new barges boat. With *Venta* we had to carry out a complete overhaul and Herbert Smeed and I made her a new rudder and sprit. In fact I am sure that they were the last new rudder and sprit to be made at the Conyer yard. While I was visiting the *John and Mary* at Upnor after the WWII I had an opportunity to go aboard *Venta* which was moored nearby. I looked over the stern to see if the rudder was still as good as when made; it had weathered the years well.

When *Venta* came to us she was owned by Captain Harvey, whose son had just joined the barge as Captain. I remember that the aft cabin was grained and varnished completely, looking fit for a King's stateroom. After the new Captain had been aboard a few days I went below and was amazed to see that all the cabin seats had been scraped and scrubbed white, but I never ventured to ask why and have been wondering ever since. Finally *Venta* was painted and blackleaded. When she went away she looked as if she had just come new off the ways.

We 'doubled' *Waveney* in about 1937, when she was then the home of Commander Crick. I well remember doing this job as it was in mid-winter when it was snowing most of the time, but the work was

Waveney, the cruising home of Commander Crick and his family was doubled in the winter months, a task hindered by frequent snowfall. 'Doubling' is the process of adding an additional skin of timber to the outside of the hull, often done to ageing barges to extend their life.

rewarded by a party after we had finished the job. We converted *Mermaid* to a yacht barge about the same period of time, for Dr. Flint.

Even before the last war we had a number of barges in to be converted to motor power - after the war there were many more. The last full-sized barge to be slipped was the *John and Mary*, for 'Nobby' Clarke and his wife Molly. While winching *John and Mary* up into the shed on 'double slips' the winch broke so she was left with part of her stern overhanging the campshed until a new winch was obtained.

John & Mary with almost a third of her length unsupported over the campshed after the winch had broken when hauling her into the shed in 1947. The barge outside her is the *Sunbeam* which, like the *Mermaid*, was built in 1888, also a product of John Howard's prolific Maldon yard. Beyond *John & Mary* the spars and sails of *Waveney* can be seen.

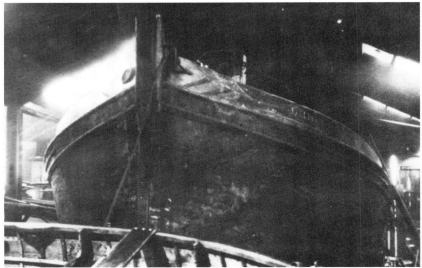

John & Mary finally in the centre shed at White's Conyer yard.

The non sailing barges, which we built two at a time about every three months, were built much the same way as their earlier sailing sisters were. The design of course differed slightly, but they were built to approximately the same dimensions. These craft were either swim headed lighters or canal craft for the Lea Conservancy, for which there was still a demand. This was the principal work on which I was engaged.

When I joined the yard, so much of the trade was new to me; I was given a week in which to get used to the system of working. I found that I was continually being called on to give a 'pitch up', which was the term used for a lift of anything heavy, and all things in barge yards were heavy! From that I came to realise that there were no light jobs in a shipyard, or if there were the 'elders' claimed them. I was beginning to learn all about it and one of the first things I learned was that the building sheds were wind tunnels in the winter and ovens in the summer, and that the autumn and spring were the best time of the year for working. But at least I was to find that life was never dull.

My first week at the yard proved not too difficult. I was put to work cleaning the saw-mill and the saw pits of saw-dust. The pitch pine dust was bagged up for a local butcher, most of the other sorts being sold to a local farmer to spread in the bottoms of his chicken huts. From this I progressed to oiling the large cramps and bottle-jacks and cleaning up in general.

The next job put paid to the nice new overalls which my mother had bought me. I was to look after the 'Hot-Stuff' coppers. These were enormous tar coppers where a mixture of tar and pitch was boiled until it was 'fit'. It was my task to dip a stick into it occasionally, then when it was cold, the Guv'nor would press his thumb into it. If his thumb stuck to it, it was ready; if it did not then it was too hard and more tar had to be added, or if too soft more pitch added, until it was just right.

This 'Hot-Stuff' was used for stuffing planks. After a plank had been made ready to fit it was stood on edge on trestles between two pegs, then the men would shout for 'Hot-Stuff', I would put the mop into it and take it along to whoever wanted it. The shipwright would then run the mop full of boiling hot tar along the plank edge, being sure to put plenty on, after which I would help him to put a layer of elk hair onto the 'Hot-Stuff', pressing it down firmly. After it was all covered with elk hair the mop was again run over the hair, soaking it with boiling 'Hot-Stuff'. All hands then gave a 'pitch up' and the plank would be set down with wooden wedges, gradually, until it showed a tight joint, about $1/16$" of compressed hair and 'Hot-Stuff'. Then the plank would be spiked, later to be bored for treenails, wooden fastenings, always pronounced 'trunnels'.

I graduated from this to the boiler house which served the 'Kale' or steam chest. This was about 65 feet long x 3 ft x 2 ft: The planks which required bending were put into the 'Kale' and I had to steam them for about 4 to 6 hours. It had a vertical boiler which burnt wood edging from the planks, which I had to saw up with a worn out hand saw. When the planks were ready to bend, I had to undo the

Two barges being built side by side for the Lea Conservancy at White's Conyer yard, 1936. They were for use on the Lea Navigation which runs from Limehouse on the River Thames north to Hertford. The barge under construction in the foreground is the *Enfield*.

The stern of a barge planked up.

The outside of the barge after planking up. The Elk hair can be seen protruding from the joints. This was never cut off until completion as it kept the air away from the joints preventing them shrinking. Working under the bottom cleaning off the tar and hair was a filthy job and not for anyone who suffered from claustrophobia. It was an arm aching and neck stretching job. The tar and pitch which fell on your body stuck your clothes to your skin.

'Kale' door, stick my head into the steam and hook a large pair of pincher tongs onto the plank required, which would be marked on the end. The men would then pull on a rope which was attached to the tongs, and draw the plank out, then lift it onto their shoulders. This plank would be taken in and bent around the framing with shores and cramps and left to cool off until morning. We built two barges at a time and worked them up together as near as possible. This usually required us to steam twice a week.

Once a week Arthur White would come down by rail and taxi to see progress. George Gates, the Guv'nor, was yard manager like his father before him. One day Arthur White came up to see me and asked the usual questions like 'How are you getting on here?' He then put his hand in his pocket and gave me half a crown telling me to buy tools with it. George Gates saw this and afterwards told me to consider myself honoured as Arthur White had never been known to do this before.

The fore-end of the Lea barge *Leyton* framed up ready for planking. The shipwright's adze is on one of the barge's floor timbers.

We were working with a small staff at the time, there being only George Gates, Herbert Smeed, Jack Baker, Stanley Hawkins, Ronald Austin, John Baker, 'Duffle' Carrier, Fred Austin, and myself. Fred Austin was the sawyer. 'Duffle' Carrier, the blacksmith, was as strong as a lion, deaf as a post, but for all that he had a gentle nature and to see him swing a 28 lb. sledge hammer was something that I shall always remember him by. He was killed in a motor cycle accident. I had become so attached to him for the help he had given me when I started work at the yard, that on the morning when the 'Guv'nor' told me he had been killed I openly shed tears. I was then 17 years old.

Sometimes it would be my task to go to the lower wharf with the 'Guv'nor', sorting out planks and holding the chalkline while he lined them out. It amazed me how he could throw a line and hit a prick mark 6 inches from the straight, anything up to 15 ft away from him. I later learned to do this and was astonished how easy it was when you knew how.

At other times I had to go bottom sawyer. My uncle Fred, 'Tiny Austin' was a first class pit sawyer and he would take his spiling board to a flitch, mark his spiling on both sides and when after cutting, the knee or cant frame would be put into its place it needed hardly any adze work to fit it. I may explain here that a flitch was an oak plank, usually between 4 inches and 8 inches thick and often grown to shape for cutting. It was working with my uncle Fred that I found out that the bottom sawyer's job was just to throw the saw back up to him and never pull it down. Neither did the top sawyer push down as the saw was carried down by its own weight. He guided it. So in fact a bottom sawyer had all the hard work to do.

Boring trunnel holes was another odd job. These were bored with a $1\frac{1}{8}$" pod auger which used to raise blisters and make the arms ache. Then we had to mute the trunnels and then drive them in by the hundreds. I think the worst job was boring the long bolt holes through the knees, sometimes in an awkward position so that the auger handle had to be a loose fit to slide through, because there was no room to turn it. Steel pilot pointed bolts were driven into these long holes $\frac{1}{16}$" greater in diameter than the holes, to ensure a tight fit. These were then cut off with a cold chisel and rivetted over a washer. All these bolts were made up in the forge as they were needed, it being difficult to estimate the length required until the holes were bored. The length was taken by a fit rod passed through the hole so that it hooked to the outside, then a mark was put on the rod, level with the inside, and then measured after removal from the hole.

Not all our work was on new craft. We always had one or two barges under repair, or being doubled. This latter job was also classified as being dirty work, especially if the bottom was to be doubled. The barge would be blocked so that we could work underneath. The blocks were on a chalk and flint bottom which had to be luted as the tide went out. The lutes were $1\frac{1}{2}$ inches thick elm boards, 2 feet 6 inches by 1 foot, with a hole in the centre to take a long handle. These were pushed to and fro until the tide had left the area, taking the 'stirred up mud' with it. As soon as the tide had left the hard we used to get our boards, which we could either sit on or lie on, these boards had to be worked under the barge to where we were to work. This was a wet, dirty job, as the water continually dripped on to us. Our old clothes, which we kept on purpose for the job, were always wet through. What made that job really troublesome was the fact that raw sewage from the houses in lower Conyer ran out of a pipe almost in the centre of our hard. This was a constant source of annoyance and one day, being fed up with these unbearable conditions, I rammed a sack tightly into the end of the pipe; this stopped the nuisance and was appreciated by one and all. Unfortunately, I forgot to take the sack out before I went home, and the next morning the people living low down were getting a flowback through their toilets. The manholes were all taken up and the pipes were rodded but no cause could be found. It was not until the tide went down that we realised what had happened, so we carefully removed the sack and released the offending matter, saying nothing to anyone about it.

Before we doubled any barge's bottom we had to refasten it: this meant driving 5 inch and 6 inch spikes upwards and the last two hits of the maul would make contact with the wet mud, clinging to the very water-logged planking and our faces would get spattered, and by the end of the tide we needed a bath. After refastening, we had to level the bottom off. This was done by using short handles in our adzes so that we could sit on our boards and chop away. Only enough was trimmed off that we could put doubling on it between tides, the doubling being

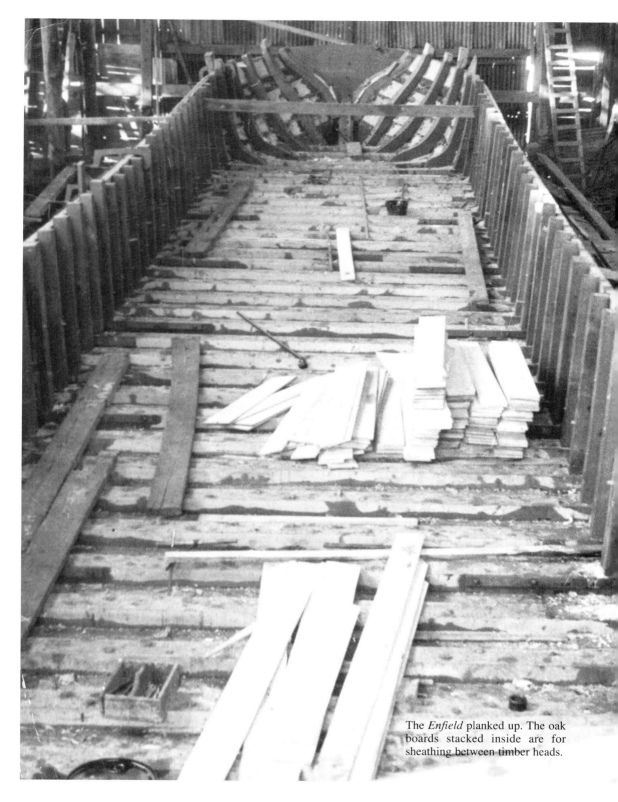

The *Enfield* planked up. The oak boards stacked inside are for sheathing between timber heads.

1 to 1¼ inch thick elm, with a layer of barge felt in between soaked in 'Hot-Stuff' and spiked up with 4 inch spikes.

The blocks on which the barge sat were shifted each tide to a new position, so that the planking could be continued. Perhaps one of the worst jobs came near the completion of a new barge. This was removing the stocks from under the barge, and then we all went underneath, the youngest in the middle. I often had visions of the barge falling on me, and it was quite some time before I became used to it. Once underneath, with our two inch chisels and a pot of waste oil, we started chiselling the waste tar and hair off the joints. This came off in a long strip and little bits stuck to our faces and got down our necks where the heat from our bodies melted them and joined our underwear to our skin. It got in our hair, and of course stuck to every part of us. After the hair was all cut off we had to scrape it to the outside and wheel it away for burning. I decided it would make good boiler fuel so I made a heap of it for the next time we steamed. I have never seen such black smoke in all my life. Fortunately it blew across the creek,

The newly launched Lea barge *Rye* outside the sheds in 1935. Despite her utilitarian dumb barge role, she still exhibits a delightful shear and purposeful appearance. Although *Rye* might seem out of step with the Lea Conservancy policy of naming their craft after places on the Lea, the name refers to Rye near Hoddesdon, through which the navigation passes. It was at Rye House, hard by the Lea, that the Gunpowder Plot was hatched by Guy Fawkes.

but the wind changed suddenly and the next thing was that Conyer disappeared in this black, thick smoke. One lady in particular, never forgave me. She had her washing hanging on a line directly in the path of the smoke. I had never raised steam so quickly before or after: flames came out of the boiler chimney three foot long only 6 feet from the boarded sides of the sheds.

Soon after this episode I blacked out Conyer again. I had lit the fire under the tar copper and had to fill it with new tar, which had to be watched because it would boil over until the oil had all boiled away. Unfortunately I was called away, I thought for a short time, but it took longer than I imagined. The telephone rang and the 'Guv'nor' went to answer it. It was from the boat yard across the creek, wanting to know if we needed any help to put out the fire. In my absence the copper had boiled over and run into the firebox adding extra fuel which caught alight, and the whole thing went up in a sheet of flame. We managed to put it out, but the copper had to be rebuilt...

After cleaning the bottom off, the next job was to put the slip under the new barge. Originally double slips were used, but by the time I started work we launched with a single 12 inch wide slip, placed centrally with a fall of 6 feet in 90 feet. This took two days for two of us to put under, and another day to pack it tight to the bottom. While we were doing this, the barge was supported on four blocks, two for'ard at the start of the runs and two aft in the same positions.

On the day of the launch large bottle jacks would be placed aft to lift the barge off the blocks, which were taken out and the barge would be lowered onto the slip. For'ard the blocks would be replaced by dog shores, four each side, with folding wedges. When the time came for launching, a man would be placed each side and when the 'Guv'nor' gave the word, the folding wedges would be knocked out as quickly as possible, which lowered the fore end onto the slip and away she would go. After sweeping the runner from under the barge she was tied up and we would all go into the Ship Inn where Arthur White had laid on beer and sandwiches. The rest of the afternoon was spent

The blacksmith's shop is the building to the left of the Ship Inn, in front of the bargeyard shed. A barge with a broken spreader lies alongside the Quay. This picture was taken after 1911 as the brickfield chimney completed in that year can be seen beyond the barge.

clearing up the floating packing from under the slip and replacing the end of the shed. The next day would see the stocks being set up for the next barge.

Launching was always at midday or thereabouts, then when we went to the Inn for beer and sandwiches it counted as our lunch hour, so we had not really been given anything. I remember once that a tide did not reach its height at midday, so we went back and launched at night by paraffin lamp light, getting home at four in the morning, but back to work at seven as usual.

On occasions we boys had to help in the blacksmith's shop, next to which stood the machine shop. The first time I entered this dim, low ceilinged building, I could think only of a museum, the machines being some of the oldest I have ever seen. An enormous cutting and punching machine for steel work stood centrally: this had obviously been worked by steam power years before. It had a monstrous fly-wheel to which had been fixed a handle 3 feet long. It would take three boys about two minutes to get the fly-wheel spinning, and after one cut through an inch bar it would almost stop, so one can imagine what a morning's work was like.

Another source of torture was a large pillar drill which had an overhead fly-wheel. We used to do all the drilling on this machine, the drills being made by the blacksmith out of old rasps and files. It used to take a day to drill a 2 inch hole through a gudgeon iron. The drill needed frequent sharpening and the swarf came away like dust. All the apprentices were christened on this machine, being tied to the overhead flywheel and spun around. This was later banned when one was almost killed. There was also a fly press punching machine which almost tore our arms out. This was used for most holes in metal, except where strength was required. These were punched out hot by the blacksmith.

Next to the machine shop was the paint store, where we mixed all our paint from oils and powder. This was ground in a machine, again turned by hand. The walls of the paint shop were 2 inches thick in paint where for years, paint brushes had been rubbed out. I chopped a lump off one day and could see at least two hundred coats displayed in different colours.

I did mention that there are not many interesting jobs today. On reflection I don't think the youth of today would want to work as hard as we had to; although interesting, it was strenuous. We started at 7 in the morning and worked until 7 at night and I have known the time when I have gone home, had a wash, and sat down for a meal, and my mother has had to wake me up to eat it. However, it did me no harm. The main reason for having to work so hard was that all the barges were built for a price, so the quicker you finished them the bigger the share out at launching.

In building and repairing craft I came to know many of the skippers and mates of the barges and sometimes their owners. Some barges were regular visitors, like Colonel Bingham's craft, coming up, one after the other to be attended to. I think it was 1935 or 1936 that Captain George Feint came up the creek in *Castanet* to take over the *Bankside*. Later, after *Castanet* had completed her refit a new skipper came to take her away. I did not see Captain Feint again until I went to a meeting in Sittingbourne about 1973. Looking around I recognised his face. He saw me looking at him and came over and the first words he said to me were 'Don't I know you? Didn't you once work on *Bankside* at Conyer?' We had both recognised each other after 37 years. That to me was satisfaction.

Chapter 8

The Conyer Built Barges (The John Bird Era)

There is no doubt that boat building of a sort has been carried on, at, or near Conyer for centuries. We know that Hoy boats carried fruit and vegetables to the markets, returning with household goods and various goods ordered by local people. These Hoy boats were later replaced by Hoy barges. There must have been quite a lot of these Hoys sailing, and at least one house holder 'with an uninterrupted view of the Swale' named his house 'Cot Hoy'. This house is at Stone. Miss Russell and Miss Newman who lived there told me it was short for 'Cottage with a view of the Hoy'.

Up until the 18th. century there was no single mouth to the creek, there being a large chunk of land (of which only Fowley Isle now remains) which had five or six narrow channels leading off like the fingers of a spread hand. This must have limited the size of the vessels using the creek into Conyer.

The first builder I have record of at Conyer was John Bird, who built from 1866 to 1889. Nothing much is known about Bird, but the East Kent Gazette for 1867 does mention that one of the barges entered for the 1867 Match was owned by W. and A. Bird. The barge was *Louisa and Alice*, built at Halling the previous year.

The earliest record I have of Conyer built barges is of the *Rose* built for Osborne Dan, the Faversham flint merchant, in 1866. The *Rose's* end came in October 1904 when she struck the buttress of Waterloo Bridge and sank. This, however, does not mean others had not been built before that date, as before the 1850s barges were never registered, but I will not use this as an excuse.

There are other reasons: at the Maritime Museum, Greenwich, they have a full set of registers to examine for which you need a reader's ticket. To get a correct list of barges built, one really has to search each year's register. On my first visit to the reader's room I decided to take three registers to my reading table; in fact I only managed to search one in one day. On putting the books back on their shelves, I ran my eye over the number of registers and decided it would take me about two years to search the lot. This amount of time I could not afford, so on my next visit I had Jeremy Nesham to accompany me. With a lot of hard work we managed two more registers at various years, and by doing this we think we have covered most of the barges built in the last hundred years. The first one I traced was the *Harry*, a small barge of 28 tons built in 1868, registered at London and owned by Fred Bunting of Faversham. Also in that year the *Walter* was built, of 34 tons, registered at Faversham and owned by F. Burgess of Camberwell. In 1869 the *John & Eliza* was launched, of 38 tons, registered at Rochester and owned by E. Killick of Northfleet. She was followed by *Equivalent* in 1871, of 36 tons, registered at Faversham, and owned by Samson Dan. Her remains still lie in the East Swale near Faversham Creek.

1873 saw the *Mabel* launched, of 39 tons, registered at Rochester and owned by Rowley Richardson of London then by Turner of Rochester before the Great War. She was followed by *Jeffie* in 1874, of 39 tons, and registered at Rochester, owned by W. Richardson of Vauxhall. Captain Fred Harris had this barge for some years. That year also saw the *Lydia* launched, of 40 tons, and registered at Rochester; she also belonged to W. Richardson.

The next barge completed was also for W. Richardson in 1876, the *Phoebe*, registered at Rochester and 39 tons, which Penfold of Greenwich was still trading in the 1930's. The second barge to be launched in 1876 was the *H.C.* of 45 tons, registered at Rochester, owned by Covington of Pimlico and named after Henry Covington. The third built that year was the *Eustace*, a big barge of 76 tons, also registered at Rochester. She was ketch rigged and owned by Westwood of Millwall. In 1877 the *M.A.C.* was launched, of 47 tons, and registered at Rochester; she was another for Covington of Pimlico who did not appear to believe in wasting money on long name carving. At that time barges names were only painted on the hull and carved on the tiller bar. Another big barge was built that year, the *May Hawthorn* of 75 tons, registered at Rochester, owned by Phelande-Garrod of 19 Burrel Street, Ipswich. In later years she was named *Mocking Bird*. She was sold to Goldfinch of Whitstable, and finally broken up at Denton, Gravesend in 1950. In 1878 came the *Rosa* of 36 tons, registered at Rochester, owned by F. Bunting of 34 Cyprus Road, Faversham, later passing into the hands of Sheppey Glue Works at Queenborough. In the same year the 38 ton *Elwin* was built, also registered at Rochester, owned by Southchurch Brickfields, Essex, later owned by S. Johnson, Brompton Lane, Strood. And finally in the same year came *Ethel* of 45 tons, also registered at Rochester, owned by C. Gutteridge, and later by Parker of Bradwell, Essex, for whom she carried haystacks from the Essex farms. *Albert* and *Ellen* came in 1879, both of 39 tons, registered at Rochester and owned by A. Anderson, Randell Street, Maidstone. 1879 also saw the *Violet* launched, of 39 tons, registered at Rochester, another to be owned by Covington of Pimlico.

In 1880 came *Josephine* of 44 tons, also registered at Rochester, owned by C. Wright of Maidstone. *Amy* followed in the same year, of 39 tons, registered at London, owned by Goldsmiths of Grays, Essex.

In 1881 came the *Nellie Maud* of 43 tons and registered at Rochester, owned by C. Tolhurst of 27 East Street, Faversham. She was later owned by The Kent Stone Company and survived into the 1930s. She was followed by the *Edwin & Emily* of 45 tons, unusually registered at Cowes, owned by S. Killick of Northfleet, later by The Associated Portland Cement Company Limited in the early 1930s. Also in 1881 came the *Lizzie* registered at Rochester, of 40 tons, owned by Westwood of Millwall, and later by Robert Mercer of Rodmersham; later still by Burley's. She was burnt at Milton Creek in 1952.

In 1882 four barges were built; the first was *Dan* of 42 tons registered at Rochester, also owned by Westwood of Millwall, later by H. Cunis of Purfleet. Next came *Sarah Louisa* of 43 tons, registered at Rochester, owned by Mrs. Emily Nicholls, 30 Manor Park, Lee; later by Grundy of Southend. *John & George* followed, of 40 tons, also registered at Rochester, another for Westwood of Millwall, later by G. Wright, 36 Plough Road, Rotherhithe. The last one for that year was the *Guy*, also registered at Rochester, of 46 tons, owned by Westwood of Millwall, later by W. Cunis.

In 1884 came the second barge to be named *Violet*, usually referred to as *Mercer's Violet*. She was 42 tons, registered at Rochester, owned by Westwood, later sold to Mercer, and ended her days hulked in Hoo Creek. Also in 1884 the 45 ton *Isabel* was launched, registered at Rochester, owned by Westwood of Napier Yard, Poplar, and later by A. Rawlinson of East Ham.

The attractive ribbon carving and decoration typical of John Bird's barges can be clearly seen on the mouldering hulk of the *Violet* of 1884, as can the name R. MERCER incised on the port side of her transom below the name ribbon. She was hulked in West Hoo Creek, this photograph of her taken in 1957.

The last barge to be built was the *Charles Hutson* of 56 tons, registered at Rochester, Official Number 94569, owned by J. Lee of Strood, later purchased by W. Smith of Framlingham in Suffolk and later still by Horlocks, the famous barge builders and owners at Mistley, Essex. She subsequently became a houseboat at Pin Mill on the River Orwell in Suffolk. She was converted in 1941 and is now derelict on the foreshore in front of the Butt and Oyster public house.

John Bird's last barge, *Charles Hutson*, seen here in 1936 when in Horlock's ownership.

Before we move on to the White built barges, I had better explain the basis of ownership details of barges written here. Because of the tremendous amount of time required to research the records, I have taken the owners names from three registers spanning the last hundred years. It is therefore quite possible that others than those I have mentioned may have owned them at different times.

All these barges were built at Conyer by John Bird, and many of them were off the register by the First World War.

Chapter 9

The Conyer Built Barges (The White Era)

Alfred Marconi White, son of Alfred White of Sittingbourne, took over the Conyer yard from Bird in 1890. The White family can be traced back to 1583. In the early 19th. century they were building fast cutters at Broadstairs. Alfred White (Senior) started up a bargeyard at Blackwall in the 1880s, where he built swimheaded barges for Goldsmiths of Grays, and it was at the Blackwall yard that Alfred Marconi served his apprenticeship.

His first barge was the *Herbert*, built at Conyer in 1890, of 43 registered tons. She was destroyed by bombs at Frindsbury in 1943. In the same year he also built the *J.E.G.* of 44 tons registered; *J.E.G.* were the initials of J.E. Gill for whom she was built. She was broken up at Rainham, Kent, in 1949. I can find no record of any sailing barges being built in 1891, but as White built swimheaded lighters and canal barges, they could still have been very busy.

In 1892 they built the *Tricolor* of 62 tons for Goldsmiths, which was still afloat at Battersea as a houseboat in 1960. This was followed

White's *Tricolor*, the third barge to be built at the Conyer yard was, at 62 tons, significantly larger than the *Herbert* and *J.E.G.* It was to be five years and seven barges later before *Tricolor's* size was surpassed, *Loualf* built in 1897 on speculation, being of 63 tons. *Tricolor* was broken up at Battersea in 1965.

An Oak ready to be moved over the saw pit.

Below: The pit sawyers at White's Conyer yard just before the WWI. From left to right, Frank Inward, still living in Teynham, Nelson Harris who lives in Rye, the late Fred Austin, the author's 'uncle' who was the head sawyer, and the late Leslie Cheeseman, who was later in partnership with Cecil Crafter in a haulage business run from the wharf at Conyer. Frank Inward has the axe which was used to trim off any awkward sprogs from the timber, Nelson Harris has the handspike used for levering large timber into place over the pit, Fred Austin is about to sharpen the pit saw, which is on the sharpening horse. Stacks of oak flitches can be seen stacked in front of the the sheds. The rear of The Ship Inn can be seen in the left hand top corner.

by *Glendower* of 37 tons in 1893, and *Siola* of 54 tons in 1894, again for Goldsmiths. *Siola* was entered in the barge race of 1894 and was placed fourth. In 1894 a second yard was opened at Faversham. *Vendetta*, 58 tons, came next in 1895, followed by the *Foxhound* of 56 tons in the same year. *Foxhound* was entered in the barge race of 1928, and was placed third in the River Bowsprit class. Around 1910-1911 *Foxhound* was burnt down to the waterline while carrying a freight of petrol. She was rebuilt and re-entered the Ramsgate Shipping and Hoy Company's service. The *Foxhound* finished her days as a houseboat and was burnt at Oare Creek in 1955.

In 1896 came the *Claxfield*, 43 tons, (namely after a place just outside Lynsted), and the *Agnes* of 36 tons. The *Claxfield* belonged to Mercer's who had their own wharf at Conyer.

Three barges were built in 1897; the *Alpha*, 42 tons built for Eastwoods. She was a handy barge which Captain Howard sailed single handed for almost two years; she was burnt at Otterham in 1950. Next came *Madcap*, 63 tons built for Goldsmiths, and *Satanita*, 50 tons, built also for Goldsmiths who entered her for both the Thames and the Medway barge races of that year. She was first in the Medway and second in the Thames, a very fast barge with a good racing record. She was, however, to be involved in a tragic accident. The Whites senior and junior held a private race to see who had built the fastest barge; White senior entered the *Victoria*, White junior entered the *Satanita*. Three other barges entered to make a race of it, this being the first time a race had been held on a Sunday, which was frowned on by the more righteous people of the day. During the race *Victoria* was hit by a squall and capsized; Mr. Austen, the owner, and Captain Webb were both drowned. The barge was towed to Northfleet, righted and eventually returned to trade.

White's three adjoining sheds fronting the frozen creek during a hard winter.

1898 was a particularly busy year, no fewer than eight barges being built. The first of these was *Kappa* of 39 tons, being built for Eastwoods, and after a long hard life in the brick trade, was broken up at Otterham in 1952. Next came *Iota* for Eastwoods' brick trade, also of 39 tons. She became a sailing yacht barge and then a house barge on the Thames, at Old Windsor. *Buckland* of 35 tons came next. There was a bit of local flavour in the naming of this barge after Buckland Farm. She was built for Mercer, passing later to Smeed Dean.

The next barge was built on speculation. My Aunt Alice Austin, who still lives close to the yard, told me that not knowing what to call her Alfred White took half his wife's name Louisa, half his own, and came up with *Loualf*. What a lovely name! It always reminds me of King Arthur's Knights who had such mellifluous sounding names. She was 64 tons, and while under construction was bought by Wilders and Carey of Essex. *Loualf's* launching day was an important one for Alfred Marconi White. It was a Saturday and at Conyer Mrs. Wilders broke a bottle to celebrate *Loualf's* launching. Safely afloat, the launching party then set off on a mad dash to Faversham where White had a second barge waiting to go down the ways at his Faversham barge yard. This second barge the *Dart*, also for Wilders and Carey was launched by Mrs. Wilder's granddaughter. In spite of having to launch both barges within a matter of an hour or so, the local newspaper reported that both launchings were most successful. The two barges were destined for the London River cement trade, *Loualf*, although she did have a race or two, never came better than fifth. She became derelict in 1936 and was burnt at Murston in 1954.

Nesta came next. Of 42 tons, owned by Woods, brickmakers of Milton, she was a hulk in Milton Creek the last I saw of her, on the north bank of Ballast Wall Reach. She was followed by *Lord Nelson* of 45 tons which was raced quite a lot. I know she had at least five second places, but I cannot find any record of her ever coming first. She ended up being owned by Arthur Wenban of Sittingbourne and was sunk at sea.

The *Lord Nelson* could claim to be the barge built in the shortest time. She was laid down, launched and raced in the space of six weeks. At that time before a barge could race she had to carry at least three cargoes, this she undoubtedly did but what her cargoes were or how far she carried them, I have never been able to find out. Even I, who knows a fair bit about barge building, find such a feat incredible in such a short time. I have heard old barge builders talk about it and there is no doubt about it. There were a lot of shipwrights employed there at that time; all three freights could have been carried on the way to the race (and they could have been any small object) being dropped off at places like Queenborough and other destinations up the Thames.

Pioneer and *Protector* were the last two to be built in 1898. Both were large, 64 tonners built for Edward Lloyd the paper manufacturer at Sittingbourne. They lay derelict for some years and were burnt together near the head of Milton Creek in 1966.

Three were built in 1899. *Northumberland* was the first. She was another Eastwoods' barge, of 43 tons. Worn out in the brick trade, she became a housebarge in 1945 and was broken up at Hoo in 1951. She was followed by the *Durham*, also for Eastwoods, of 42 tons. She was an unlucky barge, being cut down by a Dutch ship and sunk. The crew were saved and taken to Greenwich Hospital. She was salvaged, repaired and loaded with 40,000 bricks, she sat on the grid iron at Barking and sunk once again, only to be raised once more and returned to work. She became a mud barge, rigged with a small standing gaff mainsail and worked out of Halstow until 1957. Next came *Royal George* of 59 tons. She was built for the Ramsgate Hoy trade, and like most of the Conyer built barges had a good turn of speed. She passed to the London & Rochester Trading Co. Her sails were removed in 1939 and as a motor barge she was sunk in collision in 1951 and was eventually broken up at Norton's Yard, Greenwich, in 1959. Also in 1899 four swim head lighters were built, of 90 tons, for Edward Lloyd Ltd. Their names were *Ladysmith, Mafeking, Kimberley,* and *Belmont*. They were sold for £695 each.

In 1900 four barges were built: the *Sandown* of 44 tons, being given another local name, and built for Mercer. She was a housebarge at Chatham in the early 1930s, derelict in 1957 and burnt two years later. Next came the well known *Westmoreland*, 43 tons, another of Alfred Marconi White's 'flyers'. Her record is so well known that it

The sisters *Durham* and *Westmoreland* were of similar size and built about a year apart, but by the time of this photograph taken in 1957, though both were still owned by Eastwoods for whom they were built, they were in very different condition, the former sporting a rent standing gaff mainsail and relegated to the mud work, the latter resplendently kept, mainly for racing.

Durham hulked at Glass Bottle Reach, Halstow just two years later, where she was eventually broken up.

needs no praise from me. She became the property of the Thames Barge Sailing Club in 1963 and after an expensive refit got hooked up on a concrete lighter in the Medway. I went along with Lawrance Tester and Hugh Perks to see if it was possible to salvage her. Alas, the poor old girl had torn her bow completely

away. I am not saying that if large sums of cash had been available it could not have been done, but now as I write, Colin Frake has purchased the hull, towed it to Faversham and hopes to rebuild the bow section to ultimately have her sailing again.

Lancashire, of 43 tons followed, also built for Eastwoods, she was sold to Wakeley's and ended her days as a motor barge and was finally buried at Maldon. The last of that year's launchings was that of the *Rutland* of 36 tons, another of Eastwoods' 'County Class'. She was broken up at Whitehall Creek.

1901 saw three barges go down the slips. The first of these was the 'stumpie' *Warwick* of 36 tons registered, launched by my aunt, Alice Austin, who was then eleven years old. She was yet another of Eastwoods' barges which were laid up after the Second World War to await their fate. Alf White used his second name on his next barge, the *Marconi* of 43 tons. Or was she named in appreciation of the Marconi? Although she was a fast barge she never seemed to do well in races and ended her days by being broken up at Ramsgate in 1946. *Victory* was next, of 44 tons,

Lancashire under sail, light, in 1934.

at one time owned by a Mrs. Mary Pover of 54 Park Road, Faversham. She became a motor barge in 1946 and in 1960 was hulked in Shepherd's Creek.

1902 was perhaps Alf White's year of glory. He built the largest sailing barge ever built at Conyer. The *Olympia* of 97 registered tons, was built for Colonel Honeyball of Newgardens, Teynham, farmer and coal merchant, perhaps one of the most important people in Teynham at the time, whose coal business spread all over Kent.

The barge was ketch rigged and when I worked at the yard George Gates, who managed the yard, told me that she was so long that she protruded ten feet outside the shed. The sheds are 90 feet long and to this day you can still see where the shed was cut out to allow the stem through; the stem came to the edge of the road which was only a flint surfaced dirt track leading to the brickfields. Her stem head only just cleared the roof cross-ties when she was launched; she must have looked massive after the the normal run of barges. My Aunt Alice was at the launch and she told me that it was a bright cold day, cold enough to make Mrs. Honeyball

Westmoreland at Faversham, not long after she came into the ownership of the Thames Barge Sailing Club. Note the similarity of the transom shapes, typical of Alfred Marconi White's barges, on *Durham*, *Westmoreland* and *Lancashire*. More than 25 years on, *Westmoreland* still lies at Faversham awaiting completion of her rebuild following her sinking at Hoo.

have both hands in her muff. As Mrs. Honeyball stepped up to name and launch the barge, which was named after her, she handed the muff to her husband who promptly put both his hands into it where they remained until the ceremony was over. In 1910 *Olympia* was still valued at £1,800 with its insurers, still Class A. The *Olympia* was not built for speed but to carry several hundred tons of cargo each trip. Her port of registration was Faversham. She was sunk in collision (see page 64) while on passage across the Channel, a sad end to a White masterpiece.

The 50 ton *Sara*, one of the best racers ever built, followed, and up to 1963 had, in the Thames and Medway races been placed sixteen times first, ten times second, and ten times third. What a wonderful achievement both for the barge, her builders and crews, not forgetting the owners who spent considerable sums of money preparing their barge for races. Everards, her last owners, never sold her but broke her up themselves (not wishing to part with her) at Greenhithe in 1965.

James & Ann of 42 tons was the first to be built in 1903. She was owned in Faversham most of her life by Horsford, then by Cremer. She sank 3 times in collision, in 1947, in 1949, and then as a motor barge was cut down off Erith on November 1972, cement laden out of Faversham. The master and his wife were drowned.

Next to be built was the *Ronald West* of 73 tons, built for Samuel West, designed for cargo carrying and no racing. She was followed by *Toots*, 51 tons registered, built for W. Cunis who had

The 1903 Thames Barge Match was raced in one class. Two of White's barges were entered, one new that year, the other a year old. This photograph shows five of the eight entries on their way back to the finish from rounding the Mouse Lightvessel which can be seen in the distant background. To the left are White's *Sara* and *Torment* sailing home in the strong N.N.E. wind. To the right are *Genesta* and *Thelma*.

a fleet of barges with peculiar names. *Torment*, also of 51 tons, another of Cunis' barges, was next to go down the slip. She was entered for that year's barge race and came third to *Sara* which was first, the *Giralda* placed second, *Torment* only beaten by two of the fastest barges that ever raced. It was also reckoned to be the best barge race on record. What a day for Alf White, to have two of this barges in the first three!

1904 saw *Tam* of 41 tons and *Wumps* of 39 tons, built for W. Cunis, followed by *Resurga* of 50 tons, built for Samuel West. For 1905 I can find no trace of any sailing barges being built. In 1906 the *K.C.* of 42 tons was the only one built. She had finished up as a house barge by August 1962. Richard Sherren, a former actor, was fined £30 for sailing *K.C.* from Greenwich, London to Felixstowe Ferry in Suffolk in an unseaworthy condition, which Sherren denied.

1907 was an unlucky year for the yard. They had two barges being built when the sheds caught fire. They managed to save one and

Setbacks occur in any successful enterprise. On the night of Wednesday 25th. March 1907 a disastrous fire put paid to the launch of the *Dawgie* which was due to take place on the Saturday.

eventually launched it, the *Doddles* of 41 tons; her sister, which was to be badly burned, was the *Dawgie*, both for Cunis. Odd sounding names for barges, with due respect to the late Mr. Cunis, but it has been suggested they were nick-names of some of the Cunis family youngsters. After the fire the charred remains of *Dawgie* were pulled outside the sheds and for years remained there, a charred mass of timber. Following that disastrous year they rebuilt the yard and were engaged on building swim head lighters and dumb barges; in between they did a lot of repair work and rebuilding.

In 1912 *Doddles* capsized while crossing the Maplin Sands. She had a crew of three, all brothers, whose ages were 14, 18, and 21; they were all drowned.

The year of 1913 saw them again working on a sailing barge, the *Ashingdon* of 59 tons, built just before the First World War for the millers at Daren Mills, Dartford. She was back in Conyer in the mid-thirties for repairs. Owned by Peters until the early 1950's she was the last barge owned at Southend. She then became owned by Mrs. Blackden's parents, and once again had a link with Conyer. The last I heard of her she was a house boat in 1970 at Chiswick.

Right: *Ashingdon* at the Southend Corporation Jetty in May 1949 when she was operated by Peters of Southend. In less than three years after this picture was taken she had become a housebarge at Chiswick.

Top left: *Ashingdon* just after her launch. The owner and his family are on board. Also on board are Alf White and his wife, and Ben Lewis the foreman shipwright.

Bottom Left: The Shipwrights, Sawyers, Blacksmiths and the Apprentices on board *Ashingdon* after she was launched on 27th. February 1914. Standing, from left to right: Charlie Carter, Frank Jeffrey, Fred 'Tiny' Austin, Jack Baker, Alf Whitehead Snr, George Cole, rear George Gates Snr, front Austin Harris, Charlie Cooper Snr, Joe Cadwell, unknown lad sitting on windlass bit, Ben Lewis, Gus Taylor, T. Baker. Sitting, from left to right: Jack Harris, Herbert Smeed, George Gates Jnr, Anderson, Frank Inward.

The outbreak of war in 1914 signalled the end of barge building at Conyer. Two were constructed that year; the first was the *Joy* of 56 registered tons, built for Rankins, the millers at Stambridge in Essex. She was sold for conversion to a yacht at Saltcote in 1956 and when last heard of she was in the South of France. The very last Conyer sailing barge was the *Annie Byford* of 54 tons, for John Byford of Poplar. I worked on her in 1936 when she came to Conyer for repair and refit. She was eventually sunk at Erith laden with cement. After the *Annie Byford* was launched, the shipyard was put on work for the Admiralty making floats for the submarine defence booms. These were baulks of timber bolted together to make multiples of 6 ft. cubes; they were built on Richardson's Wharf and, when finished, some were lifted into the water by Richardson's steam crane, others tipped in, to be towed away by tugs to Sheerness.

No more sailing barges were built, but work continued on canal barges and lighters, and also repair work. I can remember the names of the last four barges we built for the Lea Conservancy, which were the *Enfield, Rye, Leyton* and *Latton*. These were followed by a big swim head lighter which White built on speculation, but sold before we had finished her to a beer company which named her *Expe*. We finished her just as the WWII

The penultimate sailing barge to be built at Alfred Marconi White's Conyer yard was the *Joy* for the Rankins at Stambridge Mills, Essex, at the head of the River Roach.

One of the anti-submarine boom floats is tipped into Richardson's Dock to be tied to others of their kind then towed to the Royal Navy docks at Sheerness.

A family photograph of the Whites taken c.1888. Four generations are pictured. Back row L-R are Harold White, William Frederick White, the housekeeper, Archibald White. Middle row L-R are Louisa and Alfred Marconi White, William Sandwell White, Alfred White and Kate, his third wife. Front row L-R Samuel Septimus White, Thomas Mills White, Susan Kate White, Ernest Edward White. The infants on Alfred Marconi and Louisa White's knees are not identified.

started during which we came under the Ministry of Supply and built seven swim head lighters for the gunpowder works at Waltham Abbey. Our experience with the Lea Conservancy was useful as Waltham Abbey was on the Lea Navigation. These were the last barges to be built; only barge repair work and yacht repair was done after that.

Chapter 10

The Coastguards

The Kent Coast Blockade was formed by the government to fight the enormous organised 'free trade' or smuggling gangs, which built up during the long Napoleonic Wars with France. Originally the seventy-four gun ship *H.M.S. Ramillies* had been anchored in the Downs, the sailors coming ashore each night to patrol the coast. But this was not a good idea, as there were gaps when each shift changed. So round 1818 it was decided to move ashore, using the Martello Towers where they were able to, and building new stations where necessary. The Kent Coast Blockade was split into three divisions: we are only interested in the Left Division, as it concerns Conyer. The Left Division was located as follows: Shellness and Harty; a vessel at Elmley Ferry; Milton; Bathhurst; Sheerness; Scrapesgate; East End Lane; Hensbrook; Warden Point; Leysdown; Conyer Creek; Beresford; Pioneer;

The isolated creeks and inlets off the Swale were ideal for smuggling.

Faversham; Graveney; Seasalter; Fish House; Whitstable; Tankerton; Swalecliff; Herne Bay; and Bishopstone. We can be sure that the Coastguard Cottages on the hill in Conyer were built between 1818 and 1829. On September 27th. 1829, an advertisement appeared in the Kentish Gazette listing the stations, with this wording:

TO BAKERS
Such persons as are willing to contract for supplying the Officers and men of His Majesty's Ship Ramillies for the undermentioned places...

The list starts with Conyer and ends with Bishopstone, obviously for delivery reasons. It continues:

The contract to be supplied by some person residing at Canterbury; Herne Bay; Whitstable; or Faversham, who will not be allowed to perform his contracts by agents.

AND TO BUTCHERS
For supplying good fat well fed Ox Beef.
Tenders to: - JOHN QUINNELL, Purser. Left Division Blockade.

The Coastguard cottages are without doubt some of the oldest buildings in Conyer, being built before 1829. They are now all tenant owned and have some of the best kept gardens in the village. They are pictured here in 1976.

Civilians were rapidly replacing the sailors. In 1831 the service became known as Preventive Water Guard, and in fact it was not called the Coastguard until 1864.

There is no doubt that Conyer was a bad area in relation to the size of the station, with its armoury and Customs House, which stood close to the shipyard, and was pulled down about 1947.

Up to 1939 smuggling still went on in Conyer. I was questioned several times by Coastguards about various boats that used the shipyard. I knew at least one which was engaged in smuggling. Eventually it was caught off Ramsgate.

One of the customs' officers who visited Conyer daily had to pass a farm which brewed cider; it appears that he could not pass this place without sampling the brew, and by the time he reached Conyer he was pushing his cycle instead of riding it. He would go into our forge to sleep it off. On waking he would ask if anything had come in on the tide. Time and tide waits for no man!

Of the last two smugglers caught at Conyer one turned King's evidence, was released, prospered and became rich; the other, who had been sent to St. Helena, returned and lived for many years in an old boat off the creek, and was drowned one stormy night when the boat overturned.

There was always a Revenue Boat at Conyer. Charles Igglesden in Vol. XXII of 'Saunter Through Kent with Pen and Pencil' tells a delightful story of meeting an old native leaning on the wall of the Ship

Looking up the Creek during the winter of 1939. The bottom right corner of this picture is the location where the Coastguard Revenue Boat was moored during the period they were stationed at Conyer Creek.

Inn smoking his pipe. In answer to his questions 'Was this a smuggler's haunt?' the native replied: 'I can tell you this was the 'ottest 'ell for smuggling that my grandfather ever knew, and 'e ought to know and 'e did. The revenue men 'ated their work 'ere. It was unhealthy - you see; the mud's deep and it's a nasty death to find yourself being pushed under, and under, and the mud in this creek's very slushy. No; I'm told that one revenue officer must have fallen in accidental like, for 'e disappeared - smuggling still went on.'

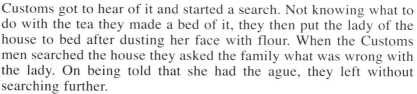

Talking to a Conyer born friend over a pint in the local, he told me how one of his relations, many years ago, had an enormous amount of smuggled tea in his house. This had been smuggled into Conyer by devious routes. The Customs got to hear of it and started a search. Not knowing what to do with the tea they made a bed of it, they then put the lady of the house to bed after dusting her face with flour. When the Customs men searched the house they asked the family what was wrong with the lady. On being told that she had the ague, they left without searching further.

Not so many years ago there were families living in Conyer who still had contraband lace that had been smuggled in via the Creek.

Going back to the year 1730, the farmers had to raise farm wages to the princely sum of 1/6d per day, which was perhaps a reasonably good wage as this was mainly an agricultural area. Even so the farmers had great difficulty in finding enough workmen to work their land. The people were finding it paid better to run smuggled goods, such as tobacco, tea, brandy, silks and lace. Consequently the farmers, finding it hard to make a living themselves, likewise turned to 'Owling' (the smuggling of wool out of the country to France), which was at that time illegal.

If you wake at midnight, and hear an horse's feet,
Don't go drawing back the blinds, or looking in the street,
Them that ask no questions, isn't told a lie,
Watch the wall, my darling, while the Gentlemen go by!

Rudyard Kipling

Chapter 11

Mercer's Wharf

Mercer's *Lizzie*, built by John Bird at Conyer, seen in the early 1930s. The new frontage to Shell-Mex House, once the old Cecil Hotel, can be seen. *Lizzie* was nearing retirement and was hulked by 1936.

Mercer's Wharf was at the head of the creek, some way past the entrance to Richardson's Dock. The wharf was fed by a tramway from the Company's brickfields at Frognal; the tramway crossed the marshes and it is still possible to see the embankments where it enters the wharf. Running parallel to it was the tramway of the Co-op brickfield which also can still be seen.

Robert Mercer had his own fleet of barges, some of which were built at Conyer. The Mercer's were farmers and landowners, which gives good reason to believe that cargoes of farm produce as well as bricks were carried in their barges. Among their barges were the *Frognal, Violet, Lizzie, Claxfield* and *Buckland*. Robert Mercer lived at Rodmersham, not far from Teynham and his principal farm was at Buckland. Buckland Farm was run by his bailiff, Walter Russell, while the foreman at the Frognal Brickworks was Stephen Edned, who was to lose many of his family from typhoid in 1894.

After the brickfields closed down the wharves were unused for some time; in fact some years. They were eventually taken over by Charles Cooper who started a boat building business. This boat yard turned out some really good work. His 14 foot International was very much a winner and many of them were built. There was a complete range of boats to choose from, from the dinghy to the ocean-going yacht. Later a Mr. Harvey joined the firm, and stayed with it for many years. After he left Charles carried on alone again. When WWII started, the Sittingbourne Ship

Yacht and boat building at Mercer's Wharf Conyer which had by 1936-7 become Charles Cooper's boatyard.

Building Company needed extra space for the extra work brought about by the crisis, so they came to Conyer. Charles stayed on as manager, and a very busy place it became! All sorts of Admiralty vessels were built: cutters, diving boats, landing craft and various other sorts of special purpose craft.

After the war Charles once again took over the yard and ran it until his death in 1966. Another son of Conyer had passed on, leaving another legend, like his family before.

In 1963 I was asked by Roy Walmsley, who was at that time the landlord of the Ship Inn, to start a sailing club. This I did and in no time we had 70 members, which was at that time about as many as we could cater for owing to space. Charles rented us part of Mercer's Wharf at a peppercorn rent; later we insisted he took more. He gave us a free hand to do as we pleased and for a year we used his shed for a clubhouse; then when we had acquired enough money we bought an American Air Force bungalow which was erected on the wharf; this proved to be a perfect clubhouse, having changing rooms, etc, all under one roof.

The club operated from here for four years and enjoyed the benefits of club racing or cruising, whatever one fancied.

Conyer has always had its Regattas, even before 'Class' boats became popular; everybody who could get hold of a boat joined in the fun and some sort of a handicap was worked out. No-one really cared what his handicap was, the main object was to see whose wind he

The start of the first regatta after WWII.

Some of the members of the Mercer's Wharf Sailing Club soon after its formation. From left to right: Cyril Monday, Charles Cooper, Don Hodge, W. Edwards, David Cooper, Ella Thomas, John Ovington Jnr., Ron Brown, Gail Curtis, John Ovington Snr., Welby Curtis, Kay Sattin, Gerald Hales, Don Sattin, H. Millen, Allan Cheeseman, Allen Cooper, Anthony Sattin, Barry Edwards and Janice Monday.

could take, or if not, one would try to make Old Bert luff up and stick him on the putty. Libellous things were said to one another on passing or rude gestures were made, nothing really mattered as long as everyone had their sail. About half the fleet used to finish the course, the rest would either capsize, get stuck in the mud, or lose their mast. They were a grand lot though, some were boys, others old men; this was one day of the year when these men of differing ages were together on equal terms.

The post WWII regattas were a much more organised thing, visiting sailing clubs, schools and other organised bodies would attend.

Club members being towed home in 1962 after the wind had dropped. They are Bernard Wareing in the tow boat, A. Johnson and A. Cheeseman in first sailing dinghy, Anthony Sattin and Sylvia Mepham in the second dinghy, Ella Thomas and Ron Brown in the last. A small part of Fowley Island can be seen to the left of this picture taken from Butterfly Wharf.

Barry Knell sails his Silhouette Mk.II cruiser over the finishing line in the 1963 Conyer Regatta. A strong wind was blowing and crowds of spectators line the shore to see the excitement.

Such things as the greasy pole over the water always attracted a large entry, swimming races, rowing, sculling, children's races, were all going on while the sailing boats were out of sight; this held people's attention until the boats came back within view. There were many trophies to be won: the main one in the regatta was The Geoffrey Stevens Memorial Challenge Cup which was kindly donated to the sailing club by Douglas Edwards of Conyer, who was the late Geoffrey Stevens' cousin.

Mrs. Cooper told me that Mrs. Stevens mentioned to her that she hoped a local man would win the cup in the first year. Her wish was granted when David Cooper took first place.

David Cooper (son of the last Charles Cooper), was the first winner of the Geoffrey Stevens Memorial Trophy, and is seen being presented with it by Mrs. Ruth Stevens at Mercer's Wharf in 1964.

Mrs. Stevens was the organist at Teynham Church for many years; her husband sang in the choir at the same church; in fact they were a very musical family. I once attended the wedding of a friend's daughter at Teynham Church where Mrs. Stevens was the organist and her daughter, a friend of the bride, sang a solo. What a lovely voice that girl had! I can imagine them standing round the piano at home having a family get-together, all of them Conyer people.

Mrs. Stevens and her husband were always known as Ruth and Sid and they later took over the village shop but they had to close it when the Brickfield closed, as this had much reduced the population, many of whom had moved away to find other work.

Eli Head's punt gun was fired from the wharf to start the village Regattas many years ago. It is now owned by Ron Sillcock who purchased it from Eli some years before he died.

When Charles Cooper died in 1966 the boatyard was sold and we were asked to leave as the site was wanted. The club now operates from Sittingbourne, and is known as the Sittingbourne Sailing Club.

Chapter 12

Disaster and Celebration

Like most parts of the East Coast, Conyer had its worse floods in living memory on that fateful night of 1st February, 1953.

I shall never forget that Saturday night. There was a dance at the Tin Chapel, or to give it its right name, St. Mary's Hall, which stood at the top of the hill just beyond the Brunswick Arms.

Debris carried by the tidal surge surrounds the sailing barge *Henry & Jabez*, her gangplank hanging steeply from her side, the flood waters having engulfed the land.

There had already been a high tide warning at midday but the high tide did not materialise. Then at 11.45 p.m., someone came into the hall to tell the people who lived at Lower Conyer to go home via the washback (a path at the back of the houses which was used by all the local people in daylight), but quite an obstacle course at night.

By this time the water was level with Mr. Dadson's steps (the house nearest the bottom of the hill).

The head of Conyer (Richardson's) Dock. The shed in the centre of the picture was where the old steam crane was housed.

I knew this was an exceptionally high tide, and it had an hour still to flow. I had seen many big tides before and had rowed a boat along the road at Lower Conyer. Realising that I had never seen the tide so high as this before, I got to wondering if the local boat owners were easing off their mooring to allow for the rise of the extra high tide. It never dawned on me that the highest tide that I had seen before came to within one inch of the sea wall, and in fact the water must have been pouring over the seawall at that very moment, flooding the marshes and low lying land and driving the sheep and cattle to find higher ground.

Another view of the top of the dock. The neatly tended gardens of the barge dwellers are completely submerged.

There were about six of us at that dance who lived in Deerton Street, and at 12.15 p.m. our taxi came to pick us up. We took the marsh road home and within a few minutes that road was under four feet of water in places.

Sunday dawned and a bitter cold wind was blowing from the nor' east; most men had been called from their beds early to attempt some sort of animal rescue. It was a pitiful sight which most of us saw that morning; there were drowned sheep washed up along the water's edge, also some cattle and all the fresh water fish, but the worst part of all was the poor creatures that were trapped on high ground standing in water, some of them up to their necks with no chance of immediate rescue. Having got inside the seawall, the sea water could not get out again so we had a large inland sea covering many square miles. It was a sight that had not been seen for centuries, and one does not want to see it again. The damage was enormous. I stood there for some time just looking at the carnage the floods had wrought, unable to take it in.

There were fruit orchards only discernible by a few small branches above water. We rescued some chicken houses first and all the chickens were safe, even though their houses had been submerged up to four feet, the birds having found high perches clear of the water. Later we managed to get a boat, the wind was still quite strong and whipping up rough seas. Having rowed to some sheep which were standing on a high piece of ground, we found great difficulty in getting them into the boat, so we decided to leave them where they were. They could not have swam, their wool was already waterlogged.

In spite of the tragedy, something told me to have a good look around. I was seeing something that probably had not been seen for almost a thousand years. I was seeing what the Romans saw; a wide expanse of water between the mainland and the Isle of Sheppey, broken only by islands of higher ground, the remainder which had taken hundreds of years to reclaim and had been taken back by the sea in less than an hour.

The only outlet for the water was the one small sluice gate where the stream passed through the seawall, and so the flood water could not escape back to the sea. The Royal Engineers were sent for. They used explosives to blow large holes in the sea walls which allowed the water to leave more quickly, although it was several days before it had all gone. The holes were sand bagged each tide to prevent the water from returning. After the water had left it remained to solve the farmers' problems. Most of their livestock had gone, and they had no grass to graze the remaining animals.

Large pumps were brought in to attempt to wash the salt out; afterwards a coating of gypsum was spread over the land. Nothing would grow until the salt had left the land, and it was between seven and ten years before fruit trees were replanted.

Back at Conyer, many houses were flooded, ruining the furniture and floor coverings; many boats were sunk and a number of cars were under water; almost everyone had been affected and many claimed compensation.

Neighbour helped neighbour and the houses were soon cleaned out and dried. In a crisis like that no one seemed to remember grudges, there were only offers of help, any differences forgotten.

But the floods too were soon forgotten, with the prospect of the the Coronation of Queen Elizabeth II a few months away.

In 1953 when Queen Elizabeth II came to the throne Conyer and Deerton Street got together to celebrate the occasion. A lot of Conyer people had married and were housed at Deerton Street forming a link between the two communities. A carnival queen was chosen, Miss Valerie Mepham, at the time just eight years old. She was crowned by Mrs. G. Crick, there was a considerable number of floats in the procession which started at Banks Farm and finished at Eastwoods' sports field where the brickworks now stand.

The Conyer bus helped link the local communities at a time when car ownership was the exception rather than the rule.

Right: The programme detailing events to celebrate the Coronation of Queen Elizabeth II shows how both the land based and waterborne residents were a single community, a prize being offered for the 'Best Decorated House, Barge or Boat.'

And there was another occasion when the villagers turned out in full force, and this was when part of a film 'Raising A Riot' was being shot at Conyer with well known film stars Kenneth Moore and Hayley Mills. The local children were so well behaved that the director publicly announced that they were the best children he had ever had around in all his years of film making. Not once did he have to tell them to be quiet during filming.

The film plot required Hayley Mills to catch a fish. On the end of Hayley's line was hooked a local one griped from out of the creek at the bottom of the tide. Part of the film included a scene on a sailing barge where Hayley rescues a kitten from aloft.

The film was on location at Conyer for some time and one local lady who washed Hayley's clothes remarked what lovely costumes she had to wear in the film.

Sadly, though perhaps inevitably, there was a repetition of the disastrous flooding on the morning of 12th. January, 1978. A high spring tide coincided with hurricane force N.W. winds. In the early hours of the morning there was a tidal surge, breaching the sea-walls and creek sides. The low lying lands to the west of Conyer, past Blacketts to Tong Mill, and southwards from the head of the creek all the way to the railway line at Teynham, were completely under water. Army units from Chatham were called in a number of attempts were made to rescue the livestock trapped in the fields, but many cattle and hundreds of sheep were again drowned. The sea-wall between Luddenham and Uplees held the water at bay, but there was disastrous flooding to the eastward at Faversham, Oare, and Seasalter and also on the Isle of Sheppey. Nearly 7,000 acres of land were under water and over 2,000 head of livestock were drowned.

Elizabeth R
1953

CONYER AND DEERTON STREET

CORONATION

CELEBRATIONS

Official Programme

TUESDAY, JUNE 2nd, 1953

Hon. Sec. : A. R. BAKER
12 Eastwood Cottages, Conyer.

Chairman : Mr. A. ANDREWS

Treasurer : COMD. A. GRICK

Committee :

Messrs. R. Hodges, J. Sifleet, B. Baker, E. Norris,
T. Graydon, G. Parsons, N. Webb, S. Stevens,
A. Tyler; Mesdames W. Taylor, W. E. Edwards,
M. A. Baker (Senior), G. Parsons, B. Brown,
D. Baker, T. Edwards (Junior), G. Sattin,
F. Taylor, J. Pankhurst.

PRICE 6d.

Chapter 13

Conyer in the 1970s and Beyond

Naturally the village life continues to evolve around the waterfront and waterside activity. The village is a favourite place for yachtsmen and has two flourishing boatyards. What used to be Cooper's Boat Yard is today Jarman's Boat Yard. This yard has altered considerably over the last few years. It is now a Marina, catering for vessels of all types and sizes, with covered storage for a limited number of boats. There is water and electricity laid on, facilities for the do-it-yourself yachtsman, modern toilets, a chandlery shop which is stocked with all the essential things that are needed in connection with yachts and yachtsmen, including clothes, food, even sweets, books and charts. Yachts stored on dry land can be lifted out by a mobile crane; a masting derrick and slipway are also provided.

Moorings are to wharf or pontoons and the dredging of mud berths has been carried out for some while now. This enables the yachts to leave their berths earlier and return later, an important factor to the weekend sailor who has to arrange his sailing to suit the tides.

The usual repair and fitting out facilities are available to the yachtsman who has not the time or the inclination to do them himself.

White's Barge Yard is today Conyer Marine. The old barge yard has had quite a transformation since I started work there in the mid-thirties. For one thing the draught holes have been blocked up and the sheds look in good condition.

Conyer Marine also caters for the weekend yachtsmen, the do-it-yourself man, also with undercover storage, dry land storage, chandlery; in fact all the usual facilities which go with modern marinas. Moorings are slightly different here, being wharf or jetty, a slipway and masting derrick. Water, electricity and fuel are available.

Conyer now has a resident sailmaker whose sail-loft is in a building adjoining the Ship Inn, built on the site of the old bargeyard forge. The sailmaker is Mrs. Ursula Wilkinson, who has the advantage of having considerable sailing experience. Ursula, in fact, makes anything from canvas, and started the business because she thought the need was there. A plucky decision to make when lots of small firms are going to the wall. I wish her well.

Barge and boat dwellers in the dock in 1976. To the left is the former R.N.L.I. Lifeboat *Sentoare*, and in the distance is the former Faversham owned barge *Gold Belt*.

Another enterprise which has recently started up in the village is the building of small Dutch sailing barges by Aqua Sprint Ltd., who manufacture the 19 ft. 8 ins. long 'Friesche Tjotter'. The hull is constructed in G.R.P. (Glass Reinforced Plastic), with traditional fittings in wood.

To the newcomer the Conyer of today presents an aspect of charm and beauty, of simplicity and variety. He must be somewhat mystified, by the apparent clash between old and new. New mock-Georgian houses and town houses stand cheek by jowl with the brickworkers' cottages; retired barges lie on the mud in contented domesticity while the sleek modern fibre-glass yachts stand aloof, their rigging beating out a new message in the breeze against their polished anodised aluminium masts.

And yet, notwithstanding, he will gradually find that this seeming contrast is superficial only; that a happy blend has come about between the old and the new, the traditional and the modern.

Once an object of suspicion and curiosity, the more recent residents of Conyer have gradually been assimilated into the general life of the village. With them they have brought a breath of the wider world, introduced new ideas and in their turn added a new dimension to the life of the village.

And then there are the residents of the dock, once a busy place for the loading and unloading of barges. Today some of these barges serve the role of houseboats, making comfortable and elegant homes. Together with other residential craft, they comprise yet another facet of life in Conyer.

Over the last few years the old cottages have been attractively modernised and now make very comfortable dwellings, more than one being occupied by previous houseboat owners who came up to Conyer years ago and who have stayed ever since. Several will tell you of how they came to Conyer for a quick look at the place, decided to stay for a week or so, and years later are still here. Other cottages welcome holiday-makers for a week or a fortnight. Who knows, these same visitors may well make Conyer their home sometime in the future.

What is it about the hamlet which attracts and holds people? Is it the peace and tranquillity? The beauty of the surrounding countryside and the charm of the place itself? The friendliness and the variety of the residents? Or is it the very ettle of the place? Perhaps one should not isolate any one factor but merely accept the blend of all these.

Finally, the interim development; the council houses which, in their turn have extended Conyer outwards, yet enriched it inwardly, perhaps giving the hamlet a stability which it may have been in danger of losing.

Again, more lifeblood has been transfused into the village upon the reopening of the brickfield. The final aspect of village life which has enjoyed a resurgence is that of the boating activity. Several hundred sailing boats are now shared between

The graceful Howard built *Mermaid* was once the home of Dr. and Mrs. Flint who had her converted to a yacht barge in 1937, but by the time of this picture, taken in the mid-1970s, she was a static house barge.

All that remained of the *Mermaid* in 2003. The cost of maintenance of such craft is prohibitive, and many of the few that remain afloat will suffer the same indignity. By 2004 all trace of her has gone.

The *Persevere*, pictured here in her berth at the head of Richardson's Dock in 1971 is, in 2004, the sole survivor of the many ex. sailing barges which came to Conyer once their trading days were done.

the two boatyards and tales of adventure on the high and low seas may often be heard by the modern intrepid mariner over his pint in The Ship, much of which one sometimes feels is colourfully embellished for home consumption sometime in the future, or for the benefit of the occasional Sunday dinner time drinker out for a run in the car with the wife and family. They will sit over their Babychams and in wonderment and awe listen to the latest tale of adventure and daring across the English Channel or down the East Coast, given forth by any one of the several real characters in the yachting fraternity.

And yet Conyer has seen the preparation of more than one trans-oceanic and near round-the-world voyage. Not only is it the haven of many, but also the jumping off point for more than a few. At the time of writing one craft is nearing completion for such a venture, while another is half way across the world. Bon voyage to both and to those others who no doubt will follow. Perhaps here lies yet another key to the secret of the fascination of Conyer: that in a society daily beset by mundane consideration and ruled more than ever by soul-sapping machines, a man can still find adventure and a feeling of satisfaction in successfully having a cruise, however short.

Situated as it is at the end of a narrow country road, Conyer must, despite these changes, remain a haven, a hideaway where folk can let their souls catch up with them, a place of peace and friendliness, where people can still smile and help one another without question and without seeking reward - a rare phenomenon today in the jungle of surrounding suburbia.

Finally, it behoves us all as lovers of Conyer, and all that it represents, to preserve the hamlet body and soul, to fight off the speculators with an eye to a 'quick buck' and with no regard for the spirit of the place.

Almost all the words prior to this paragraph were penned for the first edition of this book. More than a quarter of a century has passed by since and much has changed at Conyer. The most dramatic of these changes was the closure of the reopened brickfield, a final farewell to an industry that had sustained the community for more than 100 years. Some of the Conyer folk displaced by the closure stayed in brickmaking, finding work in Sittingbourne; other found employment at the Bowater's paper mill in the same town; a few found work on the local farms. But this was a body blow, a change which altered the character of Conyer forever.

At first the new houses which sprung up were in spaces between older buildings, and many blended well into the surroundings. But as the inexorable momentum of development gathered pace, the speculators feared in 1976 appeared amongst us in force, the new properties began to outnumber the old, the bargeyard was flattened to make way for even more expensive housing and Conyer is now very much a dormitory village, almost empty in the daytime, and occupied by many who have come from afar and commute to London or elsewhere for the means to afford their new lifestyle.

And with new development has come fencing, barring passage to all those parts of the village and waterside that were once enjoyed by all in the community. At one time I used to lecture at nearby Swaleside Prison, where many inmates were serving life sentences for heinous crimes, but I couldn't help thinking that they had as much freedom to kick a ball about as the present inhabitants of Conyer.

The Ship Inn and garden in July 2004.

Now the Ship Inn is the only surviving pub, the Brunswick Arms finally closing its doors in 2000. And to my knowledge just two of the many hundreds that make up the population of Conyer have their roots in the village. But the visitor, diligent in his or her search, may still find many clues to the proud maritime and industrial heritage of Conyer's past, the dock itself, part of the cement works, the tramway embankments and, of course, the profusion of brick rubble hiding just below the surface!

Appendix 1

Some Conyer Built Barges that Raced

The Thames Barge Matches were started by Mr. William Henry Dodd in 1863, a man who made a fortune out of collecting and disposing of refuse. He had started life as a ploughboy in London before that great city had sprawled itself along each side of the River Thames. When he died on the 27th. April, 1881, he left no less than £100,000, a considerable fortune in those days.

Many of the early barges which raced were swim headed, while I can find no record of any of this type having been built at Conyer, it is probable that some of the earlier craft may have been built in this fashion. This is not a complete list of Conyer constructed barges which raced, but it will give the reader some idea of the quality of the locally built barges.

THAMES RACES

1894	Champion Topsail Class	*Siola*	4th.
1897	Champion Topsail Class	*Satanita*	2nd.
1898	Champion Topsail Class	*Lord Nelson*	2nd.
		Satanita	3rd
1899	Champion Topsail Class	*Lord Nelson*	2nd.
		Loualf	6th.
		Satanita	7th.
1900	Champion Topsail Class	*Loualf*	5th.
1901	Champion Topsail Class	*Lord Nelson*	2nd.
		Marconi	3rd
1902	Champion Topsail Class	*Sara*	3rd
		Marconi	7th.
1903	Champion Topsail Class	*Sara*	1st
		Torment	3rd
1904	Champion Topsail Class	*Resurga*	4th.
		Marconi	8th.
1905	Topsail Class	*Resurga*	4th.

1928	River Bowsprit Class	*Foxhound*	3rd
1931	River Bowsprit Class	*Sara*	1st
1932	River Bowsprit Class	*Sara*	1st
1933	River Bowsprit Class	*Sara*	1st
1933	Staysail Class	*Marconi*	3rd
1934	River Bowsprit Class	*Sara*	1st
		Lord Nelson	2nd.
1934	Restricted Staysail Class	*Westmoreland*	3rd
1935	Bowsprit Class	*Sara*	2nd.
1936	Bowsprit Class	*Sara*	1st
1936	Staysail Class	*Satanita*	3rd
1936	Special Staysail Class	*Westmoreland*	3rd
1937	Champion Bowsprit Class	*Sara*	1st
1937	Staysail Class	*Westmoreland*	3rd
1938	Bowsprit Class	*Sara*	4th.
1938	Staysail Class	*Westmoreland*	4th.

The *Sara*, pictured here racing under the Everard flag, following her sale to them out of Horlock's ownership at Mistley.

1953	Champion Bowsprit Class	*Sara*	1st
1954	Champion Bowsprit Class	*Sara*	1st
1955	Champion Bowsprit Class	*Sara*	2nd.
1955	Staysail Class	*Westmoreland*	2nd.
1956	Champion Bowsprit Class	*Sara*	3rd
1956	Staysail Class	*Westmoreland*	2nd.
1957	Champion Bowsprit Class	*Sara*	2nd.
1958	Champion Bowsprit Class	*Sara*	2nd.
1959	Champion Bowsprit Class	*Sara*	3rd
1960	Staysail Class	*Westmoreland*	1st
1961	Champion Bowsprit Class	*Sara*	3rd
1961	Staysail Class	*Westmoreland*	1st
1962	Champion Bowsprit Class	*Sara*	1st
1962	Staysail Class	*Westmoreland*	1st
1963	Champion Bowsprit Class	*Sara*	3rd
1963	Staysail Class	*Westmoreland*	3rd

MEDWAY RACES

1897	Champion Class	*Satanita*	1st
1898	Champion Class	*Lord Nelson*	2nd.
		Satanita	3rd
1899	Champion Class	*Lord Nelson*	3rd
1901	Champion Class	*Marconi*	2nd.
		Lord Nelson	4th.
1902	Champion Class	*Sara*	2nd.
1903	Champion Class	*Sara*	2nd.
1904	Champion Class	*Resurga*	4th.
1930	Bowsprit Class	*Sara*	1st
1931	Bowsprit Class	*Sara*	2nd.
1932	Bowsprit Class	*Sara*	1st
1933	Bowsprit Class	*Sara*	1st
		Lord Nelson	3rd
1934	Bowsprit Class	*Sara*	1st
1934	Restricted Staysail Class	*Marconi*	3rd
1936	Special Staysail Class	*Westmoreland*	2nd.
1937	Champion Bowsprit Class	*Sara*	1st
1937	Special Staysail Class	*Westmoreland*	3rd
1938	Champion Bowsprit Class	*Sara*	6th.
1938	Staysail Class	*Westmoreland*	3rd
1954	Champion Bowsprit Class	*Sara*	1st
1954	Staysail Class	*Westmoreland*	3rd
1955	Champion Bowsprit Class	*Sara*	2nd.
1956	Champion Bowsprit Class	*Sara*	3rd
1956	Staysail Class	*Westmoreland*	2nd.
1957	Champion Bowsprit Class	*Sara*	3rd
1957	Staysail Class	*Westmoreland*	3rd

1958	Champion Bowsprit Class	*Sara*	3rd
1958	Staysail Class	*Westmoreland*	3rd
1959	Champion Bowsprit Class	*Sara*	3rd
1959	Staysail Class	*Westmoreland*	3rd
1961	Champion Bowsprit Class	*Sara*	3rd
1961	Staysail Class	*Westmoreland*	1st
1962	Champion Bowsprit Class	*Sara*	2nd.
1962	Staysail Class	*Westmoreland*	1st
1963	Champion Bowsprit Class	*Sara*	3rd
1963	Staysail Class	*Westmoreland*	2nd.

The end of one of White's crack racers, the *Westmoreland*. On a big tide in 1973 she had hooked her stem on a sunken lighter at her Hoo Marina berth and broke her back as the tide ebbed.

Owned, but not built at Conyer, Mr. H. Chambers' *Murton* sailed in the Thames Match of 1867. The *Louisa & Alice* which sailed as a stumpy in the same match may also have been Conyer owned.

Sailing barges were not entered for the races every year. It was a costly business preparing them, and not all owners could afford the expense and loss of capacity for the weeks that were spent smartening them up beforehand. Barges intended for a race could be away with a freight, weatherbound with no chance of getting home for race day. In fact *Sara* went twenty five years without a race. Some owners made sure their barges were available for racing, whilst others never raced at all.

Appendix 2

Sailing Barges Built at Conyer

BARGES BUILT BY JOHN BIRD

Name of Barge	Reg. No.	Port of Reg.	Tons	Year Built
Rose	?	Faversham	?	1866
Harry	56922	London	28	1868
Walter	58473	Faversham	34	1868
John & Eliza	58500	Rochester	r38	1869
Equivalent	60242	Faversham	36	1871
Mabel	67053	Rochester	39	1873
Jeffie	67072	Rochester	39	1874
Lydia	67088	Rochester	40	1874
Phoebe	74811	Rochester	39	1876
H.C.	77603	Rochester	45	1876
Eustace	90982	Rochester	76	1876
M.A.C.	78521	Rochester	47	1877
May Hawthorn	77502	Rochester	75	1877
Rosa	78525	Rochester	36	1878
Elwin	78540	Rochester	38	1878
Albert & Ellen	79891	Rochester	39	1879
Ethel	79870	Rochester	45	1878
Violet	81872	Rochester	39	1879
Josephine	81881	Rochester	44	1880
Amy	82771	London	39	1880
Nellie Maud	84376	Rochester	43	1881
Edwin & Emily	84400	Cowes	44	1881
Lizzie	84404	Rochester	40	1881
Dan	84433	Rochester	42	1882
Sarah Louisa	84437	Rochester	43	1882
John & George	84446	Rochester	40	1882
Guy	87206	Rochester	46	1882
Violet (Mercer's)	87226	Rochester	42	1884
Hilda	90972	Rochester	43	1884
Isobel	94556	Rochester	45	1888
Charles Hutson	94569	Rochester	56	1889

BARGES BUILT BY ALFRED MARCONI WHITE

Name of Barge	Reg. No.	Port of Reg.	Tons	Year Built
Herbert	97716	Rochester	49	1890
J.E.G.	97728	Rochester	44	1890
Tricolor	99915	Rochester	62	1892
Glendower	99923	Rochester	37	1893
Siola	102872	London	54	1894
Vendetta	104317	London	58	1895
Foxhound	104320	Rochester	56	1895
Claxfield	106514	Rochester	35	1896
Agnes	106518	Rochester	36	1896
Alpha	108178	London	42	1897
Madcap	108204	London	63	1897
Satanita	108232	London	50	1897
Kappa	108326	London	39	1898
Loualf	109924	Rochester	64	1898
Nesta	109926	Rochester	42	1898
Lord Nelson	109940	Faversham	45	1898
Buckland	109912	Rochester	35	1898
Iota	108327	London	39	1898
Pioneer	110014	London	64	1898
Protector	110015	London	64	1898
Northumberland	110099	London	43	1899
Durham	110107	London	42	1899
Royal George	110311	Ramsgate	59	1899
Sandown	110974	Rochester	44	1900
Westmoreland	112733	London	43	1900
Lancashire	112734	London	43	1900
Rutland	112793	London	36	1900
Victory	104950	Faversham	44	1901
Warwick	112826	London	36	1901
Marconi	114679	London	43	1901
Olympia	114453	Faversham	97	1902
James & Ann	114455	Faversham	42	1903
Sara	115858	London	50	1903
Ronald West	118286	London	73	1903
Torment	118291	London	51	1903
Toots	118344	London	51	1903
Resurga	118464	London	50	1904
Tam	118380	London	41	1904
Wumps	118411	London	39	1904
K.C.	123866	London	42	1906
Doddles	125654	London	41	1907
Ashingdon	135196	London	59	1913
Joy	136718	London	56	1914
Annie Byford	136735	London	54	1914

Picture Sources

I am most grateful to the following who have provided the photographs appearing on the pages listed. Some are from my personal collection. Those named are the source of the picture and this is often not the person who took the photograph, who in many instances is not known.

Front cover, Author; 10, Aerofilms; 14, Faversham Bookshop; 16 top, Peter Kennett; 16 bottom, Author; 17, Author; 9 top, centre & bottom, A. Bray; 19, Author; 20, Tony Farnham; 21 top, Ray Rush; 21 bottom, A.Bray; 22, Author; 24, Ray Rush; 25, Author; 26, Ray Rush; 27,Author; 30, Author; 34, Mrs. V. Webb; 36, Author; 37, Ted Beacon; 38, Mrs. G. M. Crick; 39, Author; 40 top, Mrs. V. Webb; 40 bottom, Author; 41, Peter Parrish; 42, Author; 43,Martha Head; 44, Peter Kennett; 45 top, Martha Head; 45 bottom, Richard Walsh; 46, Author; 47, The Times; 49, Mrs. G. M. Crick; 51, Author; 52, Author; 53 top 7 bottom, Ray Rush; 54 top & bottom, Jeremy Nesham; 55, Jeremy Nesham; 57, 'Nobby' Clarke; 58, Ray Rush; 64, Author; 69, Ted Coleman; 70 top, Mrs. G. M. Crick; 70 bottom, Author; 72, Ray Rush; 74, Aerofilms; 75, A. Bray; 76, A. Bray; 77 top, centre & bottom, Author; 78, Author; 79 top, centre & bottom, A. Bray; 80, Author; 82,Ray Rush; 83, Author; 84 top & bottom, 'Nobby' Clarke; 86 top & centre, Mrs. G. M. Crick; 86 bottom, Stuart Dixon; 87, Mrs. G. M. Crick; 89, Stuart Dixon; 90, Author; 91, Mrs. R. Blackden; 95, Ray Rush; 96, Ray Rush; 97, Ray Rush; 98 top & bottom, Mrs. Fred Austin; 99, Author; 101 top & bottom, Ray Rush; 102, Ray Rush; 103, Author; 104, Ray Rush; 105, Tony Farnham; 106 top & bottom, Mrs. Fred Austin; 107, Ray Rush; 108, Ray Rush; 109 top, Author; 109 bottom, John White; 110, Ted Coleman; 111, Melvin Sillcock; 112, Mrs. G. M. Crick; 114, Ray Rush; 115, Mrs. G. M. Crick; 116 top, Author; 116 bottom, S. Newman; 117 top & bottom, S. Newman; 118 top, S. Newman; 118 bottom, Melvin Sillcock; 119, Jeremy Nesham; 120 top & bottom, Mrs. P. Nesham; 122, Author; 123, Author; 125, Richard-Hugh Perks; 127 top, Author; 127 centre, Richard Walsh; 127 bottom, Ray Rush; 129, James Olney; 131, James Lawrence; 133 Richard-Hugh Perks. Inside back cover, Author; Outside back cover, Mrs. Fred Austin.

Index

Names of vessels are shown in *italics* and figures in bold refer to plates.

Index prepared by Jane Gilbert
of
Indexing Specialists (U.K.) Limited,
202 Church Road,
Hove,
East Sussex
BN3 2DJ

Jane Gilbert was once a resident of Faversham and also of Sittingbourne; Kent towns on the Swale-side creeks either side of Conyer. She used to walk the Swale shore and visit the Ship Inn at Conyer.